SCHRÖDINGER'S CAT (THIS BOOK IS NOT ABOUT CATS!)

THIS BOOK IS <u>NOT</u> ABOUT DOGS

RAPHIE KAPLINSKY

is a distinguished development economist, now retired, but formerly employed by the University of Sussex and the Open University. In 2024 he was granted an Honorary Doctorate by the University of Johannesburg in South Africa, recognising his contributions both to academia and to society at large. He has published extensively, and has provided advice to the United Nations, the World Bank, governments in Africa, Asia and Latin America, and to trades unions and civil society organisations. Although he has written more than 15 books, he regards this book as the pinnacle of his publishing career—'More fun than anything else I have written'. His dogs and family agree.

RUPERT REDWAY

tree surgeon and gardener, dog lover and cartoonist, he has had a career working with *Private Eye*, and his cartoons can now be found in the Victoria & Albert Museum collections.

THIS BOOK IS <u>NOT</u> ABOUT
DOGS

Compiled by
Raphie Kaplinsky

Illustrated by
Rupert Redway

Anthony Eyre
MOUNT HOUSE PRESS

First published 2025 by Anthony Eyre,
Mount House Press,
Mount House
23 High Street
Cricklade, SN6 6AP

Text © Raphael Kaplinsky
Illustrations © Rupert Redway

ISBN 9781912945535

Typeset in 10/13pt Plantin

Printed in India by
Imprint Press

Outside of a dog, a book is a man's best friend

(Groucho Marx, possibly)

CONTENTS

Dogs and us—so what? 9

See a man about a dog 20

Doggone 24

Love me love my dog 28

If you lie down with dogs you get up with fleas 32

Barking up the wrong tree 36

Every dog has its day 40

The dog's bollocks 43

You can't teach an old dog new tricks 48

Dogging 53

Dogs can speak, but only to those who know
how to listen 56

Raining cats and dogs 60

The factory of the future will have only
two employees, a man and a dog 64

In the doghouse 69

Dog-tired 73

A dog's breakfast 77

Hair of the dog 80

The dog ate my homework 84

The dogs of war 88

It's not the size of the dog in the fight, its the size of the fight in the dog 93

Don't keep a dog and bark yourself 97

Dog days 102

Dog whistle politics 108

Dog night 112

Dog-eared 117

Mad dogs and Englishmen 121

Dog and bone 126

Let sleeping dogs lie 131

The quick brown fox jumps over the lazy dog 136

Like a dog with two tails 141

Dogged 146

Going to the dogs 150

Eye of newt and toe of frog, wool of bat and tongue of dog 155

Mean as a junkyard dog 160

Black dog 163

Hot dog 167

A dog is man's best friend 171

DOGS AND US—SO WHAT?

IN DECEMBER 2020, a mere 11 months after the first case of Covid was identified in China, more than one million infections and 33,341 Covid-related deaths were recorded in England and Wales. By the end of 2021, the World Health Organisation estimated, there had been just under 15 million excess deaths globally as a direct and indirect consequence of Covid.

On December 22nd 2021, the UK prime minister Boris Johnson announced that there would be no lockdown over Christmas. Fearing that the feckless Johnson might change his mind (not an unknown event), at very short notice our daughter and family decided to escape to France. Luckily for them that they managed to get away. This was the month when the UK registered 2.5 million Covid infections and 4,113 deaths which were directly attributable to the disease.

But what was our daughter's family to do with their five dogs during this hastily-arranged break? No problem. Give them to mum and dad—five extra dogs to add to our own pack of three. Oh, and there was also the question of Coco, the dog owned by an ex-student—'Our dog minder has Covid and we want to go skiing in France...' That meant another dog. To which we need to add the two dogs who would accompany our son and family when they joined us for a Christmas Day meal. So, eleven in total.

In the event, as you can see from the frontispiece of this book, only nine dogs joined us for the Christmas meal since our son and family had come down with Covid. Nine dogs, all but one, golden and white labradoodles. The bonus for us—no disappointment over the wrong presents; no family conflict. What could be a better way to spend Christmas Day while the pandemic seemed intent on closing down the whole world?

So that serene occasion got us thinking. How is it that dogs can be such a comfort to us? And, how is it that we can be such a comfort to them? Well, before we get to those issues, and in fact before we get to the substance of this book (which is not about dogs), here is a brief recounting of some of the dogs in our lives.

I, Raphie, was born in South Africa shortly after the WWII into a privileged white family. At that time the barbaric apartheid system of racial division, exploitation and violent oppression of the country's majority in South Africa was being intensified. Our family lived in a white ghetto, serviced by servants, gardeners and delivery staff who were legally excluded from living in our locality because they were not white. (The legal definition of white included placing a pencil in someone's hair. If it did not fall out, the person was a non-white). My family had a long history of resisting apartheid. My uncle was one of the last Labour Party members of Parliament, was a partner in a legal firm which mentored Nelson Mandela and Walter Sisulu during their legal apprenticeship, and was credited in Mandela's autobiography with assisting him to evade arrest when Mandela was on the run from the security police. I too was a political activist and had to flee my country of birth to escape arrest and solitary confinement. But that is another story...

What is relevant to this book (which, as you will soon discover, is not about dogs) is the relationship which we and our neighbours had with a community of dogs as I was growing up. Virtually all of the houses in our street had one or more dogs. In that era, the dogs lived outside in a community of dog-packs. Sometimes there were fights within each of the packs; at other times, the packs would square off against each other. But essentially they led a peaceful life, more concerned with coping with the occasional bitch on heat than confronting rivals for territory. They had fun too, and especially enjoyed chasing after the horse-drawn carts that delivered milk on a daily basis. Our house was at the very tip of a rather sharp crescent and as my brother reminds me, the cart would come up one of the legs of the crescent and then turn down the other side past the back of the house. Well before the cart reached our house there was a cacophony of sound as the group of dogs further down the street was chasing the cart. When the cart reached the limit of their territory they pulled back and our gang of dogs took over. There might be a brief scuffle at the point of 'handover' when it was the turn of our local pack to take up the herculean chase, but that was incidental. On one occasion the neighbour's rather stupid bulldog, Bruce, was seen to take a massive lunge at the rubber tyre of the cart and cling on to the point where he kept being turned round and round by the wheel. Bruce was indestructible and survived this and numerous other scrapes including feeding himself on a pile of building stones.

At first our family did not 'own' any of these local dogs, although Monty would regularly turn up at evening mealtimes, initially sitting obediently on the porch and then subsequently wheedling himself into the dining room to be fed scraps from the table. For a while we were naïve enough to think that he was indeed 'our dog'. But we then discovered that Monty had an internal clock and knew accurately when each of the local families would eat their dinner, managing to insert himself into each of these families as 'their dog'.

Monty converted us, perhaps 'civilised' is a better word, and after our sister who was allergic to dogs (and to her brothers!) left home, Alpha arrived. He was a small, long-haired black and white dog, uncannily like the Greek dog we recently adopted in England (see below). Monty's act of civilising us meant that Alpha rapidly became an in-house and intimate member of our family. His speciality was to join whoever of the troubled sons was sitting on the sunlit stair-well either reading or mourning their tragic adolescent fate (or both).

Now, *my turn*, Cathy speaking! Before we explain why this book is not really about dogs, here is a brief recounting of why dogs have been ever-central to my life. As a psychotherapist, I am particularly interested in the role of the emotional attachment between humans and animals and especially their healing capacity. My family were certainly animal lovers and though I was unaware of it at the time, my older brother remembers that our mother had a baby pet elephant that occasionally came into the house, with a servant in attendance to scoop up its poop. This was in Rajasthan in India, where I was born. My father, a doctor, was in charge of the large hospital and our hospital-supplied house was also very large, with 27 rooms. My brother remembers it as a kind of castle. I have an old grainy film recording the capture of the poor baby elephant which had been lured into a pit. My parents also had a mongoose which would sit on my father's shoulder but if my mother went near him it would peck at her.

I was born in 1947, two weeks after India became independent and at the time of the partition of India and Pakistan. The country was erupting with ethnic conflict and my parents were desperate for me to be born before independence so they could 'make their escape'. But I was already revolutionary *in utero*, so hung about for two weeks in order that my parents witness some of the devastating consequences of the imperial rule in which they had participated. Now I often wonder what happened to the elephant? It could still be alive and I frequently admonish my husband that if he really loved me, he would take me back to India to try and find our old pet.

My birth was thus inextricably linked to the birth of India and Pakistan and also the occasion of a massive family wrench. In order to help with this period of turmoil and a new-born baby, my family employed a young woman from Goa called Yvonne La Porte. I imagine we clung to each other as we travelled by ship to South Africa where she lived with us until I was four. Then she left for England and we later moved house. All this would of course have been very traumatic for me. So, whoopee, I was given my first dog, Sonya, a sweet Alsation bitch, to be there for me and to heal the pain. She certainly did and I loved her dearly. She was allowed on my bed and we were deeply emotionally connected. Then, another trauma many years later when my mother died rather suddenly. My father, beside himself, decided we must move house again and restart our lives. Sonya was 'given away' without my knowing and to this day, it is heart breaking to think about it. Of course, Sonya would have been healing for me while I mourned my mother. Instead, I had to mourn her as well. Who knows what happened to her. It still hurts.

So much for our (Raphie and Cathy) personal histories with

This Book is NOT

dogs. Fast-forward to our married life in Kenya and then England, an era when dogs became central to our lives, when they moved from the garden, to the dining room, to the lounge furniture and then to our beds. Over more than five decades we have loved and lived with eleven dogs. Eight of these were 'rescued'. One was left behind in Kenya when we returned to live in England, two are still with us and with one tragic exception, seven lived to a ripe old age of fourteen or older. The tragic exception was Ella (which means 'come' in Greek) who found us on a Greek island. She was running in the middle of the road as if trying to catch up with a car. We stopped to check on her. She jumped in, charmed us and that was it. Ella was driven across Europe, arriving with a soft-toy rabbit, which our current dogs continue to adore. She was loved by all the neighbourhood but she soon sickened. As a puppy on a Greek island she had been bitten by a sand fly and had contracted leishmania, surfacing in a painful, protracted and incurable disease. We still mourn her and have a framed picture of her with an accompanying quote from E. B. White: 'A really companionable and indispensable dog is an accident of nature. You can't get it by breeding for it. You can't buy it with money. It just happens along.'

One of the adopted dogs—the wonderful matriarch Sophie—arrived pregnant (no-one had bothered to tell us when we adopted her) and then had 11 puppies in our pantry; the next was the abandoned Smudge who was found on a dog-walk by one of Raphie's colleagues ('why not ask Raphie to have him?'). And of course we provide a temporary home to the family dogs of holidaying family and friends—cue forward to Christmas 2021 and the frontispiece of this book (which, remember, is not about dogs…).

All of this personal history, and perhaps especially the joyous conflict-free Christmas of 2021 has led us to think about the relationship between humans and dogs. How is it that these four-legged creatures have become central to our extended family and to the families of our neighbours? This question got us reading and we discovered John Bradshaw's wonderfully informative book, *In Defence of Dogs*. Bradshaw was director of the Anthrozoology Institute at the University of Bristol and specialised in the relationship between dogs, cats and humans. *In Defence of Dogs* was a *Sunday Times* and *New York Times* non-fiction best-seller in 2011 and has been translated into ten languages. So, if anyone is to blame for the book you are about to read, it is (unknowingly) John Bradshaw's fault. His book, based on both his extensive personal research and the research of many collaborators, helped us to understand the centrality of dogs to our own lives, and why it is that they proved to be such wonderful Covid-lockdown family members.

The explanation goes as follows. It is often asserted that dogs are direct descendants of wolves, and that wolf communities are characterised by strict hierarchy, conflict and the quest for domination. None of this is true. Whilst it is true that dogs and wolves share 99.6 per cent of their genes, this is not because dogs are descended from wolves, but because both dogs and wolves are descended from canids (the Canidae family). Canids originated in North America around six million years ago. At some time in the past the two species went their separate ways (see the picture opposite). About one and half million years ago, these descendants of canids had spread across the globe. It is also not true that wolf packs are dominated by hierarchy and the search to be what is mistakenly called 'top dog'. That may be true of wolf packs living in close proximity to human settlements, but in the wild, wolves (and especially their relatives, African wild dogs) are essentially cooperative animals.

Bradshaw explores an especially important characteristic of dogs which is central to this book (which in fact is not about dogs). This concerns their relationship with human beings. Over the centuries, dogs and humans have grown ever closer. Initially, dogs lived on the outskirts of settlements and survived by living off the scraps and discards of their human neighbours. They were widely viewed with disdain, seen as a carrier of disease and filth. But as human settlements grew, dogs became increasingly useful to their human neighbours, warning and guarding against intruders, becoming integral participants in hunting parties and even 'soldiers' in wars. And then as societies became richer, the human need to exploit

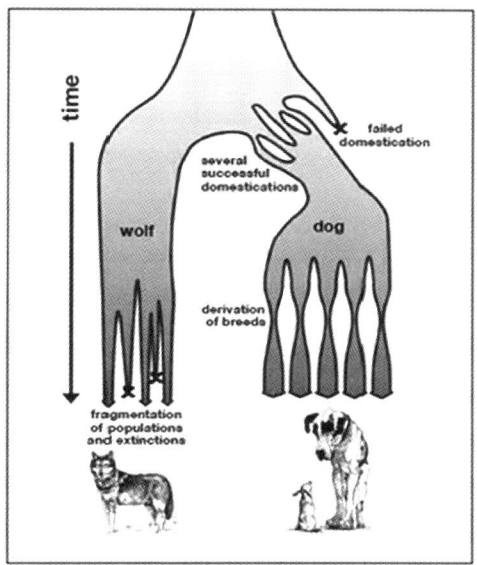

Bradshaw's chart of the evolution of dogs

dogs as useful 'economic citizens' diminished. Urban society did not need to hunt, and there were other ways of achieving security (door locks and substantial buildings). And gradually, dogs entered the home. Chinese emperors used Shih Tzus as bed warmers and Napoleon's wife Josephine slept with her pug bed-warmer every night.

The cooperative nature of the dog species and our need for emotional contact meant that humans and dogs became ever more intimate. Stroking a dog releases endorphins in humans and that helps to calm and de-stress us. It also releases β-endorphin (beta-endorphin), oxytocin and dopamine which are neurochemicals involved with positive feelings and bonding. When humans and dogs sleep in close proximity they often seem to dream (rapid-eye-movement sleep) in harmony. Thus, through a combination of 'selective breeding' (did we select the dogs or they select us?) and changes in our lifestyles and needs, dogs and humans have developed an intimate, synergistic and loving relationship. Of course this is not true of all people and all societies. In many communities and households dogs continue to live outside and are considered dirty. But in all societies and all income groups, a large number of dogs have civilised their human companions. For them, our Christmas dinner might be unusual, but not altogether surprising.

Bradshaw rounds-off his wonderful account of the evolution and nature of dogs with three conclusions. First, dogs are essentially cooperative creatures; hierarchy and the quest for dominance is a second-order characteristic. Second, dogs are acutely aware of what is happening around them, but humans often miss this since we are caught in our own species-specific means of communication. We talk with words, we may be unusually good at thinking about and planning future events. But many of our senses are way poorer than those of dogs. For example, dogs have about four times more hearing-sensitivity than we do, and are particularly alert to high-pitched sounds. Unlike dogs, we don't 'think' with our noses. A dog's sense of smell is between ten thousand and one hundred thousand times more acute than that of humans. We don't use some of our body parts (mouths, ears and tails) to communicate, and although we see more colour than dogs, we can't see around corners or in the night. As Bradshaw observes, 'I do not suppose your dog has ever been bothered by the colours you have chosen to decorate your house, but his or her delicate nose was very likely insulted by the odour of the paint.'

The third major conclusion which Bradshaw draws from his research, and the conclusion which underlies this book, is that dogs have developed an especially symbiotic relationship with humans. The dog's primary friend is the human, rather than other dogs. Even when there are a number of dogs in the home, the dog's principal loyalty and kinship is with their human owners rather than with other dogs in the pack.

All of this, and especially the last of Bradshaw's observations, explain what this book is about. That is, so central are dogs to our lives that they have come to be suffused in our language. After a cursory search, we have identified more than 60 idioms/aphorisms in the English language which draw on the metaphor of dogs. But even though we are concentrating on the English language, we have observed the use of the dog metaphor in a number of other languages, including the romance languages, German, Greek, Mandarin, Arabic and Hindi.

So we can now get to the substance of this book which, as we have mentioned, is not about dogs. It is about the English language. We have researched the meanings of 38 idioms. Perhaps you won't be surprised to learn that many idioms have more than one meaning. In each case we have also searched for the origins of the aphorisms. We have sometimes found a single point of origin, but often so ubiquitous are dogs in the lives of humans, that the same or a similar idiom has developed in more than one language. And then, we crowd-sourced short anecdotes which in some way illustrate each of the idioms, or are in some way sparked by one of the idioms.

The crowd-sourced authors have a wide range of experiences. They include novelists, researchers, psychotherapists, retirees, dog-groomers, actors, artists, mothers, fathers, siblings, children, students. Their brief was to provide an anecdote which was in some way unexpected or humorous and sometimes involved social comment to draw off, or to illustrate, the idiom. The anecdote could be personal but that was a matter of choice. Consequently, there is a great variety in the illustrations which are included in the book. But, we believe, each is in one or more ways insightful. And we hope you enjoy reading them.

So now that you know that this book is not about dogs, but about the English language and about human behaviour, here are a few health-warnings before you whet your appetite. First, unlike John Bradshaw whose book is based on deep research, most of the anecdotes in this book have what might be termed a 'loose association' with the facts. This does not mean that individual authors have consciously sought to invent reality, but rather that this is not the central intention of our enterprise. For readers who want to chase up the sources of the description of each of the idiom's meanings and histories, we do provide a list of our sources, almost entirely web-based [https://anthonyeyre.com/this-book-is-not-about-dogs-sources/]. In the same spirit the reference to the number of mentions of each of the idioms is drawn from Google's ngrams site which scans printed sources published between 1500 and 2019 (https://books.google.com/ngrams/); Nichole Kaplinsky has been instrumental in compiling this information, and we are very grateful to her for doing this. The graphs are meant to be fun rather than an accurate reflection of the changing popularity of each idiom.

In other words, Dear Reader, we hope you have fun as you plough through this book. Perhaps you might provide your own anecdotes and wish that we had asked you to contribute your story? But we do not know who you are and anyway, there would not be space to include everyone's fascinating reflections. And perhaps if any of you are teachers, you might ask your learners to go through the same or similar journeys. Can they track down the origins and meanings of particular idioms? And how about them offering a story of their own?

Each of the contributors to this book had a great deal of fun in composing their contributions. We also learned interesting facts about the evolution of individual aphorisms and the complexity and nuance of the English language. And in most cases, exploring the character of individual idioms helped us to a better understanding of ourselves and the world around us—even if we don't see as well as dogs in the night, hear as acutely as they do and have an extremely primitive sense of smell.

Cathy and Raphie Kaplinsky
Barcombe Mill, UK.

THE DOGS

SEE A MAN ABOUT A DOG

IT'S AN awkward situation. You are in discussion with someone who you like or someone who you do not wish to offend (or even perhaps someone who you both like *and* do not wish to offend). But there is something which you urgently need to do which might surprise or offend this person. It might be an urgent need to visit a toilet, or that you have to place a bet on a horse or a greyhound before the race starts. Or perhaps you desperately need an alcoholic drink. How do you slip away without divulging where you are going? It's simple—you just say 'excuse me for a moment, I just need to see a man about a dog, it shouldn't take long' and then, to use a dog-related metaphor, you scuttle out rapidly with your tail between your legs, hoping that no-one has taken offence. And if they have taken offense, too bad. At any rate, its incumbent on your listener to not press you for details on which 'dog' you are going to see and where it is.

In the mid-19th century the idiom sometimes also involved seeing a man about a horse, but that has fallen into disuse. During the prohibition era in America, seeing a man about a dog was used specifically in relation to slipping out for an illegal drink. More recently, in the late 1990s Newcastle Brown Ale (the most widely sold drink in the UK) had an image as the working man's drink. In Newcastle upon Tyne the beer was nicknamed 'dog', so that going to see a man about a dog specifically referred to going to the pub.

This idiom probably originated in the play *The Flying Squad* written by the playwright, actor and impresario Dionysius Lardner Boursiquot. It was first performed in 1866. In an awkward situation, the character excuses himself by saying 'Excuse me Mr. Quail, I can't stop; I've got to see a man about a dog'. Boursiquot had a troubled life. He was born illegitimately in Dublin in 1820 and was indirectly related to the Irish Guinness brewing family. As a teenager he had an affair with his employer, Arthur Lee Guinness, a senior member of the brewing family and was paid handsomely to go his own way. He married three times, and for a time was a

bigamist. Boursiquot was a large personality in the theatre world in London, New York and Australia and had a close association with the world of alcohol, including of course through his affair with a Guinness. No surprise, then, that the idiom which he seems to have created—or at the very least popularised—associated 'seeing a dog' with popping out for a discrete drink.

And what a dog

IT COULD have been the wart under his left eye or perhaps the sinewy finger that poked towards her as he made his tedious point—but there was something, or maybe a few things, about this Lord Bagglesby character she just couldn't abide. Was this what the famous debutant ball was really like?

She had imagined being whisked around the room, her fabulous ball gown swishing behind her, until she came face to face with THE ONE. Her one true love. If being pinned to the wall whilst boring Toffs spat tiny crumbs of canapés in her face was a night on the town, her sisters were welcome to it. Cindy began to wonder why on earth she had made such an enormous fuss about coming. Her corset was digging into her ribs and her feet ached from wearing the sequin studded stilettos—they were definitely too big and rubbed as she walked—and she longed to sit down for a minute. Her time here tonight was limited, she hadn't forgotten the one rule. Uber at midnight. Time was far too precious to be stood here, in pain, listening to the entitled opinions of boring old Bagglesby. How could she get away?

In her periphery vision, over his shoulder she became aware of a finely suited figure walking with conviction towards them. Oh please, not another of these ego inflated lords who thought it was their god given right to preach at her. But no, as the figure got closer she realised it was in fact a woman parting the people to approach them. Her dark hair was cropped closely and her sparkling green eyes were iridescent against her dark brown skin. She was dressed in a beautifully cut tuxedo suit and in one hand she held a cigarette holder aloft and in the other she clutched a quite adorable fluff ball of a dog under her arm. Her gaze was fixed on Cindy and it didn't waver as she stood there in front of her smiling. Their eyes locked. Cindy felt her stomach lurch and a shot of adrenalin coarse through her limbs making her cheeks instantly flush and her skin tingle. What was happening? Who was this alluring individual? Bagglesby seemed completely unaware as he droned on and on.

'Shall we dance?' interrupted the mysterious stranger and cocked her head for Cindy to follow her onto the dance floor.

They twisted and boogied like the best of them. Cindy had no experience of dancing in a ball gown but opposite this lady she felt loose, free-limbed and full of rhythm. She kicked off the stilettos and felt the cool floor under her stockinged feet. A magnetic energy vibrated between them and as the band played into the night their bodies gave in to the rise and fall of the tunes. Even the little dog seemed to love being swung and swayed as they grooved together. Cindy had never felt such joy, such connection.

The band finished their set to riotous applause and as the crowd burst *into cheers, the stranger leaned forward and kissed Cindy on the cheek. Then, crouching down she picked up one of Cindy's discarded high heels, gave her a wink, and was gone.*

Cindy strained to catch sight of her on the crowded dance floor but out of nowhere old Bagglesby jumped in front of her blocking her view. 'There you are my dear! It is 11.58pm, would you like to share my uber? Maybe come back to mine for a nightcap?'

'Terribly sorry' she said, her chin held high. 'I need to see a Woman about a dog'. Trembling with rebellion, remaining shoe in hand, she ran towards the exit. To her stranger. Perhaps, to the beginning of the rest of her life.

Saskia Butler, actor and writer
Barcombe, UK

Boursiquot's introduction of this idiom seems to have had little impact in the literary world during the 19th century. The idiom shot to fame during prohibition in the USA during the 1920s, falling into relative obscurity after alcohol was legalised. After the 1980s there was a sharp acceleration in its use—too much alcohol? A surprising rise in etiquette? An explosion in the number of men suffering from prostrate problems? Or perhaps that a larger number of prostrate sufferers were venturing out to social occasions?

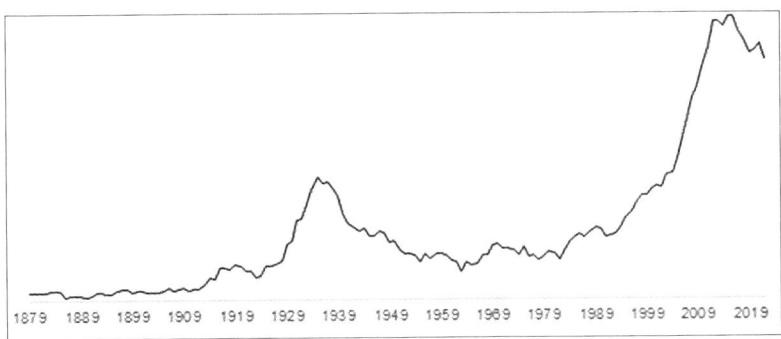

DOGGONE

'DOGGONE' is an idiom which is used to describe something which is unfortunate or regrettable. There is a touch of irritation in its use, but this is generally of a mild tone rather than a cause of intense displeasure. So, for example, 'doggone' has a similar flavour to expressions such as 'hang it', 'dammit' and 'goddamn', or in a quaint British form, 'a pox on it'.

The idiom is most commonly used in American English, particularly in the southern American states. Because of its widespread use in American popular culture, many believe that it had its origins in the US, and in the second half 19th century. However, its ancestry pre-dates its adoption in the US. The Scottish phrases 'dagone', and 'dog on it' were first recorded in 1826. Some believe that it was a derivative of 'goddamn' or perhaps 'dog on it', phrases no doubt developed to avoid profaning delicate Scottish religious sensibilities. It is even possible that it developed as a derivative of 'gone to the dogs' which as can be seen from another entry in this book lacks a religious heritage. For most of the 19th century, the idiom was used in the forms of 'dog gone' and 'dog on', but now 'doggone' seems to have triumphed the linguistic spelling struggle.

A DOGGONE FULL CIRCLE

November 24th

I spent the first years of my life in the mid western United States, in Bloomington, Indiana. This was the 1950's and although Bloomington was liberal compared to the surrounding terrain, it was also quite Christian. My father taught at the university and his mentor, a proud atheist who'd come to Bloomington more than a decade earlier, told us that, contrary to explicit Biblical injunctions, people used to throw stones at him when he walked to work. Swearing was a shocking occurrence back there and then, rare for adults and absolutely forbidden to children.

This Book is NOT

'Doggone it' was the acceptable substitute for 'goddamn it' (and 'doggone' for 'goddamn'.) I heard the phrase often until, at age eleven, I moved to California and never heard it again. I'm having trouble remembering what kids in California did say. Probably 'jeez,' which perhaps is a shortened form of 'Jesus' or else the more innocent contraction formed from 'gee whiz,' which also may derive from 'Jesus' but through the improbable route of 'gee willikers.' Only the person using the phrase can know for sure how innocently it is intended.

Forbidden words began to appear in my own speech in high school, the religiously profane first, the scatological arriving later during college. I cleaned up when I had children, only relaxing my efforts after a memorable conversation with my daughter when about fourteen. She had referred to someone, I forget who, as a 'b-word'. I said that b-word was objectionably coy; since we all knew exactly what she meant there was no point in not saying it. Be careful what you wish for. 'She's a fucking bitch', my daughter said then. I was shocked by the words but more so by the fluidity with which she spoke them. Clearly this was not her first 'fucking.'

By their high school days, my children and their friends were using 'fucking' as an adjective interchangeable with 'very.' As in, it's fucking hot out, I'm fucking tired, don't be so fucking stupid. Eventually they had children of their own and the pattern repeated; their own language all cleaned up until the day it became clear that the game was already lost. By then such language was creeping into movies and television and every other goddamn space. But for a period of several years, the only person in our family using bad language was me. Inadvertent, of course, force of habit. 'Grandma!!' my startled grandchildren would say. The bad habits we pick up from our children...

I don't know if the enormous spread of profanity over my lifetime is good for society as a whole, or bad, or indifferent. One study suggests that swearing has a positive physiological effect, reducing stress by providing an outlet. Apparently, you can work out harder and longer if you swear vigorously while doing so. But I've also seen the suggestion that casual swearing has led us to a more violent society, since the words no longer serve as a warning, a way of communicating that someone's anger is nearing volatile levels.

And perhaps, as one set of words loses the power to shock, the search for ones that still do leads to the truly offensive language of cruelty—racism, anti-Semitism, homophobia, misogyny, etc.

At the very least, we've become less imaginative. What swear word today has the surprise, the juice, of 'dadburned' or 'dagnabbit?' Say what you will about Spiro Agnew's insult to leftists as 'nattering nabobs of negativity'. At least some effort was put in. It's original. It's memorable. Today's version is Donald Trump saying someone has a 'fat, ugly face'. He can't even be bothered to word-smith it so that he sounds older than five.

And me? I plan to bring back 'gadzooks,' even if I have to do it all by myself.

November 26th

Coincidentally, after an absence from my life of almost sixty years, this very morning, I heard the word 'doggone' again. I was driving to the grocery store to pick up the necessary ingredients for my actual dog's anti-diarrhoea diet, her special Thanksgiving Day dinner having produced nothing to be thankful for. I was listening to the radio when 'Been Wrong so Long,' a track from Walter Wolfman Washington's posthumous album, Feel So At Home, *came on. All of a sudden, he's singing. 'I've been wrong for so doggone long'. What a lovely line! And 'doggone' is not in the usual lyric. Walter must have thrown it in there for me. Just when I needed it most.*

Karen Joy Fowler
Booker Prize Short-listed author and winner of numerous awards
Santa Cruz, USA.

This Book is NOT

References to 'doggone' suggest that its use coincides with eras of economic frenzy and crisis (before and during the boom-and-bust of the depression in the 1930s and the global financial crisis of the early 21st century). If this half-witted association were indeed true, this would be surprising, since it is unlikely that mass unemployment and poverty would only elicit such mild displeasure.

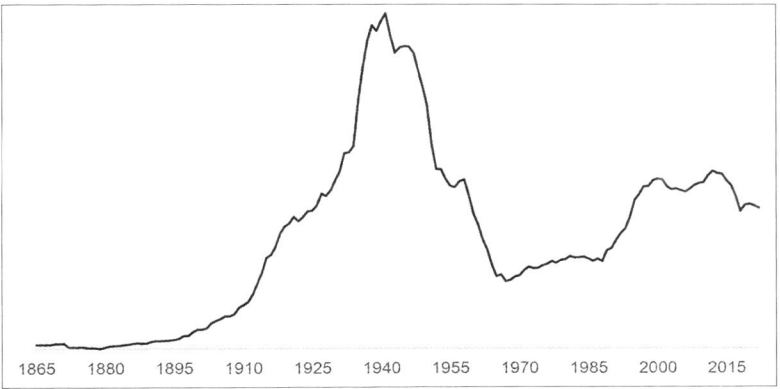

LOVE ME LOVE MY DOG

WE ARE ALL AWARE—or perhaps more accurately, most of us are aware—of our shortcomings. There are aspects of our behaviour which are less than perfect. We may be rude, we may be thoughtless, we may have annoying habits—'why is she always late? Why does he snore loudly? For heavens' sake, pick up your clothes!' But that is just who we are, and for one reason or another we cannot change. In which case, take me as I am—'love me, love my dog'.

The message that we need to be loved despite our faults is found in idioms in Latin (*Quo me amat, amat et canem meam*), French (*Qui aime Pertrand, aime son chien*) and Spanish (*Quién bién quiére a Beliram, bien quiére a su can*)—if you love someone, you will like all that belongs to him. The use of the dog-metaphor *love me, love my dog* to describe this plea for understanding in the English language is first recorded by John Heywood in 1546.

In those distant days, dogs were not household pets; they lived peripherally to humans, were fed scraps and were generally dirty and unkempt. But, the idiom goes, they were still loveable despite all of these faults. So if you are unkempt, have slovenly habits, snore at night and don't pick your clothes up, you are still loveable and don't let your friends and partners forget that.

Pete Shelley's 1973 song *Love me Love my Dog* speaks to his need to travel and the costs this has on his relationship. He knows it's destructive, but pleads to be understood, including in the refrain:

> When I leave this town today
> Lord, you know I'll miss you
> Baby, I won't kiss you
> You'll only make me wanna stay
> And though it's hard to say goodbye
> Can't you see it's over
> Guess I'm just a loner
> Heading on his way
> And I tell you now, love me, love my dog

There is always hope

I FOUND HOPE on a website called Preloved. I was going to become her third owner. It was instant love. Her owners said they wanted her to go to a new home because she was left alone for most of the day and hated being on her own. I personally think it was the £900 cash they wanted for her, but to me it was money well spent.

I took her back to London, where I live and went straight into work dressing a celebrity at ITV studios in Wembley. As I didn't want to freak Hope out and leave her in my flat alone, I took her with me. After smuggling her into my client's dressing room she gladly sat on his lap whilst he had his hair and makeup done.

Our adventures began and I decided to smuggle her into as many places as possible. She loved it—she was with me and was not alone. And it made both our lives easier! So afternoon tea at the Ritz, dinner at the Dorchester, a private tour of the Royal Opera house, the top of the Gherkin or the cinema. She was always in my bag.

However one day I was going to the opera and knew that the ushers on the door always check your bag. I was running late and if I took her home I would be likely to miss the show. There was no alternative—I had to take a chance and try and sneak her in. As I approached the theatre entrance I realised that it was later than I had thought and the show was starting in five minutes. I waved my ticket to the usher on the door saying 'I know I'm late and I know where I'm sitting'… I was let in with only my ticket checked and no one had looked in the bag.

Taking my seat in the stalls I sat down with the bag between my legs. As the lights dimmed I lifted Hope out of the bag and placed her on my lap, covering her with my jacket. As always, she was calm and quiet. I stroked her continuously. She slept happily underneath my jacket.

The show had only been going for about 30 minutes when the fun started. I felt a tap on the shoulder from a very concerned usherette who said a little bit too loudly, 'Excuse me sir but there is a complaint that you are masturbating'. Naturally, the people near me looked round horrified. They were even more anxious when I started to lift my jacket, wondering what they were going to see. Although the shape of a sausage did emerge, to their collective relief it was not the sausage they had feared. Not a penis, but my beautiful sausage dog Hope.

The poor member of staff who was given the task of confronting me was so relieved—'please please stay Sir'. So I did stay and so did Hope, snoring extremely loudly, but always in tune with the music in Poochini's fabulous *Tosca*.

Stephen and Hope Williams
Master Tailor to numerous celebrities,
including David Beckham, London.

This Book is NOT

Perhaps we all have become more considerate. References to *Love me Love my Dog* declined sharply in the 20th century and even Pete Shelley's 1973 song seems to have made little difference to our need for understanding and forgiveness.

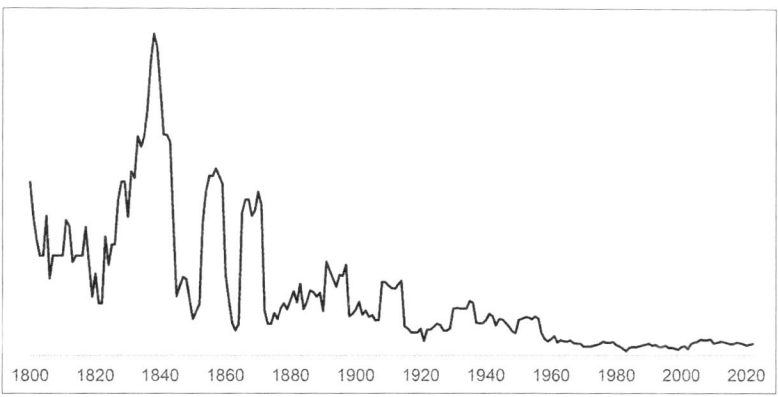

IF YOU LIE DOWN WITH DOGS
YOU GET UP WITH FLEAS

SO, DOGS are dirty. They have fleas, lots of them. And if you are stupid enough to lie down with dogs, you too will be plagued with fleas. And so it is with your personal relationships and social behaviour. If you demean yourself by consorting with unsavoury people and join in with their seedy and disagreeable behaviour, you will become infected with their bad practices.

The origins of this idiom can be traced back to Seneca the Elder, a Roman historian and writer who lived through and chronicled the rise and fall of three Roman Emperors around the time of the birth of Christ. Clearly, Seneca saw enough of unsavoury political processes to offer an admonishment against lying with dogs—*qui cum canibus concumbunt cum pulicibus surgent*, 'He that lieth down with dogs shall rise up with fleas'.

There were numerous references to this idiom in English literature after the sixteenth century. In 1573, in *Garden of Pleasure*, Sanforde repeated Seneca's admonishment 'Hee that lies with the dogs, riseth with fleas'; this was echoed in 1640, in *Outlandish Proverbs* by Herbert ('Hee that lies with the dogs, riseth with fleas') and given more flesh in 1721 by Kelly in *Scottish Proverbs* ('He that sleeps with Dogs, must rise with Fleas. If you keep Company with base and unworthy Fellows, you will get some Ill by them').

Despite these English antecedents, this idiom was popularised by the American inventor, philosopher and politician, Benjamin Franklin, who drew on Seneca's phrase in his opinionated annual publication, *Poor Richard's Almanack*. In his early life Franklin owned and traded in slaves, but he subsequently became an abolitionist and was one of the signatories of the American Declaration of Independence. Amongst his many achievements were his inventions—the lightning rod, bifocal spectacles and the Franklin stove; he also named the gulf stream. Franklin became a rich man, partly through the popularity of the *Richard's Almanack* which regularly sold more than 10,000 copies, a significant number in the eighteenth century. For a time, Franklin was president of the state of Philadelphia when he founded the University of Pennsylvania and Philadelphia's first fire department. When his brother died, Franklin gifted the mourning wife 500 copies of the *Almanack* for her to sell as a source of income. The *Almanack* was translated into Italian, French and Slovene and circulated widely in England. So there was a large audience for his annual admonitions, and no doubt after reading the *Almanack*, a good many of them stopped sleeping with their dogs and refrained from unsavoury behaviour.

Franklin has had a wide and enduring influence. For example, the sociologist and political scientist Max Weber wrote a famous analysis of the origins of the industrial revolution, tracing its roots to the promotion of frugality and enterprise in the Protestant church, *The Protestant Ethic and the Spirit of Capitalism*. Weber drew extensively on *Poor Richard's Almanack* to illustrate these defining features of capitalism. Surely one of the reasons why the industrial revolution thrived in 18th century Protestant England was because its frugal entrepreneurs held back from lying with their dogs.

AT LEAST THE FLEAS DIDN'T GET TO MUM

Some people drip with confidence: life's shit slides off them leaving no stain. Karl is like that: at 50 he can make a snot green jumper with holes look like a fashion statement. Rather than dominating a conversation he holds it, and he doesn't disagree with you, he disarms you with a lopsided smile that implies he could set you right if he chose. Perhaps deep down inside is a core of childish terror that has built up this charming armour. Perhaps...

We met during the Covid lockdown of January 2021, our paths crossing in a muddy field of winter wheat. We stopped to talk (you stopped to talk with anyone you met at that time) as his brindle lurcher, Jupiter, chased scents across the field, disappearing out of sight.

'It's cool', he assured me as I watched the spot where Jupiter was last glimpsed. 'He always comes back'.

As we waited, Karl offered me the bare bones of his life: his work as a cranial osteopath (deeply fulfilling), his weekends in a shepherd's hut in a remote patch of woodland (spiritually rejuvenating), and his deep connection to the world around him. He took me for a fellow nature disciple—why else would I be trudging the fields in misty rain without even a dog as an excuse—and invited me to an informal gathering of friends around his camp fire that evening. I hesitated, as thoughts of masks and hand sanitiser and rules flickered through my mind. But we would be outside with fire to kill the germs. So I said yes.

And there I was perched on a log, my face scorched by the flames, my toes chilled inside my wellies. I watched the faces through the smoke, distorted by the heat and animated by discussions. Karl didn't say much, and when he did, he generally contradicted the general flow, which then eddied and swirled, before the group poured their approval into this new channel. Jupiter paced behind the circle, more wolf than dog.

'They are treating us like lab rats, pumping untested chemicals into our systems'. In frustration, the woman in the bobble hat kicked out at a smoking log.

'Yeah, Doctors are not telling the truth'. This from a man in a hairy, striped jumper whose shades glinted in the firelight. 'They are controlled by the pharmaceutical industry'.

'And we know how many billions those criminals are making out of this'. Bobble Hat folded her arms and grimaced.

I had driven my mother to the doctor's surgery to get her first vaccine shot the week before and now felt guilty. She's eighty-one, with diabetes, and I had spent the last year shopping, cooking and cleaning for her so she didn't run the risk of carers coming into the house. Had I now sacrificed her health for my own selfish reasons?

Karl smiled his wonky smile and locked eyes with me for just a second. 'It is terror that is killing people, their terror machine that is controlling us. We have to release ourselves from the fear or we will be sucked into their prison'.

Jupiter paced around the perimeter of the fire and flopped down at my feet.

The guy on the next log offered me a joint that was doing the rounds. I hesitated, imagining the germs from his mouth, his hands. But was this fear reasonable? Was I being manipulated by a corporate machine? I took

After the depression in the 1930s and after the 1980s there was an explosion in references to lying down with dogs. Surely this reflects the disgust of common citizens to the rising sleaze which contributed to growing inequality and the rise of populism? The problem is that few of the very rich seem to mind being attacked by fleas…

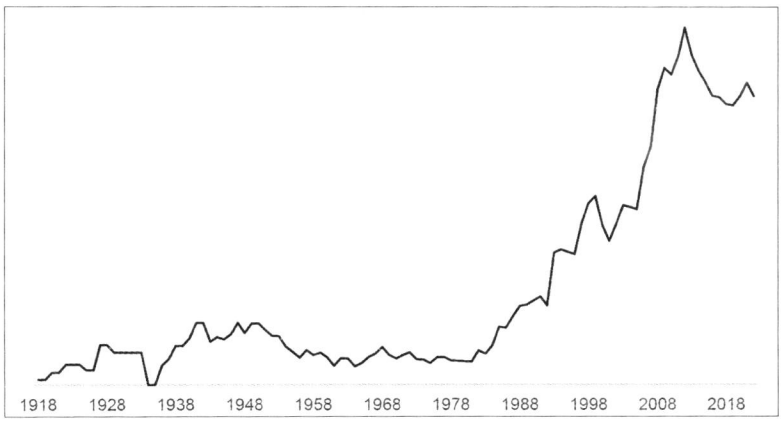

BARKING UP THE WRONG TREE

This idiom describes a waste of energy and effort because you are following the wrong path. It has a similar meaning to 'the wrong end of the stick' (which means that you are misunderstanding the situation). But 'barking up the wrong tree' has a slightly different connotation because it suggests that you misunderstand the situation because you are following a mistaken clue.

The roots to this idiom can be traced back to the practice of raccoon hunting in the southern states of America. Raccoons are nocturnal animals and were hunted by the indigenous north American populations for their meat and their fur. The breeding of dogs specifically designed to hunt raccoons can be traced back to the eighteenth century when George Washington, amongst others, adopted raccoon hunting as a 'sport'. The poor raccoons were hunted both for 'sport' and money. In 1885 a raccoon pelt was sold for 25 cents and in the 1920s, raccoon coats became a fashion item. During the great depression of the 1930s when much of rural America experienced great poverty, raccoons were hunted both for their meat and for the money earned from selling their pelts.

A hunter can catch up to ten raccoons a night. In 1985 there were said to be between 30,000 and 40,000 raccoon hunters in Michigan alone. In 2014 the *Indianapolis Star* claimed that some professional raccoon hunters earn more than $100,000 per year and that a top raccoon hunting dog would cost up to $40,000.

So, what is the link between raccoon hunting and this idiom? Raccoon dogs (of which there are six varieties) are released at night in areas which are likely be inhabited by raccoons, usually in a forest or a swamp. The dogs will pick-up and chase-down a scent, emitting a distinct and very loud bay during the whole tracking process. The tenor of the bay will vary on the freshness of the scent. The dogs will chase a raccoon up a tree and the dogs will change their vocals from a bay to a very rapid 'tree bark' (which can be up to 150 barks a minute). The raccoon is then said to be 'treed'. The following hunter then arrives and dispatches the poor raccoon which is destined to become part of a pelt.

But not all raccoons are dumb enough to stay in the same tree and they may leap to freedom. And not all raccoon dogs are skilled enough to recognise that their prey has escaped. So the misled dogs bark excitedly, making a great deal of noise, thinking that they have found the key to their owner's puzzle. But they haven't. They are merely barking up the wrong tree. And so, in the same way, if we mistakenly follow a lead in any challenge because we are pursuing the wrong clues, we too are barking up the wrong tree.

And don't keep a raccoon dog as a pet. Not only do they require a great deal of space, but they communicate with each other by scent. And don't they let you know it.

Raccoons and Zephyrs—What's the Difference?

Unlike disappointed raccoon dogs and raccoon hunters. Sometimes barking up the wrong tree has unexpectedly positive results. It is 1964, late summer, the family are returning from a camping holiday in Yugoslavia. My father is driving a company car, a deep red Vauxhall Zephyr.

There's a large case and a bulky Rent-a-Tent on the roof rack. The tent was damaged when we used rocks to weigh it down to prevent it blowing away, we now dread returning it and losing the deposit. I am worried that the tent will fall off. On the journey out a bumpy level crossing in Belgium dislodged it and it landed on the rails. Very embarrassing. I find most aspects of my family embarrassing. I'm 15.

In the Italian mountains it is pouring with rain, cool after the heat and dust in Yugoslavia. Three of us are crammed into the back bench seat, ages 15,14 and 9. We squabble sporadically over space, who has a window seat, who can wind a window, who feels sick. We argue for no reason. There are no seat belts. I can smell my mother's Max Factor face powder and my father's cigarettes. I am keen to get home, back to my job in a cafe, to a new school term and my teenage life. I look forward to telling my friends about the boy I met, embellishing the story. I'm intolerant and impatient.

Shock!

Suddenly the cars in front stop, our heavy car slides and skids on the steep wet road and crashes into the small car in front, shunting that into another vehicle which swivels and blocks the road. Shaken, my parents get out, and are shouted at. Someone calls the police.

We do not need to understand Italian to know what the police are saying, that the accident is clearly my father's fault and that he must go with them. He is put in the police cells. Someone finds us a family room in a guest house. My mother frets about what to do and how much it will cost. The car is damaged and anyway she cannot drive.

Two policemen return and begin shouting at us, not in an angry manner, more an interrogating one, but having no English they up the volume to get through to us. I notice my mother calming and smiling at them. They keep repeating 'Corps Diplomatique' and quoting our car registration '3724 CD', a Sussex plate. Little brother says 'No', my mother kicks him and smiles and nods. I'm amazed to be proud of her.

Everything changes. They are barking up the wrong tree! They think my father is a diplomat! My embarrassing father, loud, scruffy, his trousers probably secured by fraying string, with his untidy rabble of fractious children in mismatched clothes. He couldn't be less like a diplomat.

We are put in a hotel, expenses paid, apologies made, an interpreter is found (we censor what we say, suppressing little brother) our car is fixed and we go on our way.

There were more 'misunderstandings', another wrong tree, when much later the car insurance company received the claim, they assumed the invoice was in pounds not lira…

Mary Barnett, Therapist
Brighton, UK.

References to *barking up the wrong tree* reflect an explosion in the number of citations from the advent of the internet. Could that be that our ability to search for useless information on the web has resulted in us following the wrong leads?

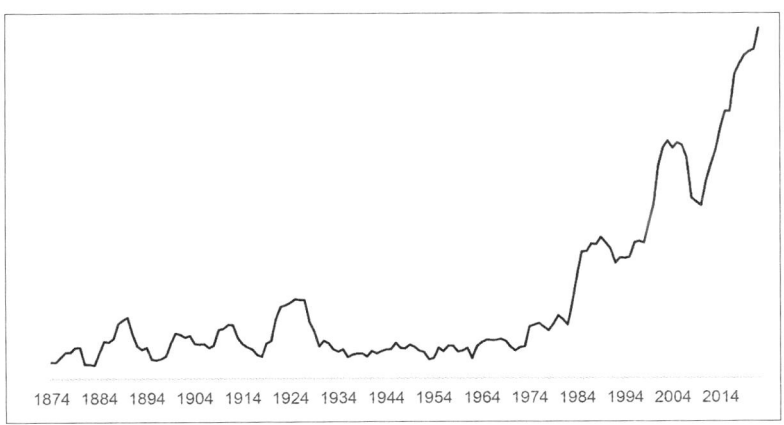

1874 1884 1894 1904 1914 1924 1934 1944 1954 1964 1974 1984 1994 2004 2014

EVERY DOG HAS ITS DAY

The phrase 'every dog has its day' means that however bad someone's plight might be, at some time in the future, the tides will turn in their favour. The idiom originates 2,400 years ago in ancient Greece. Plutarch's description in *Moralia* (95 AD) of Euripides being mauled to death by a pack of dogs concludes 'even a dog gets his revenge'. The phrase means that the neglected or downtrodden will one day obtain their revenge.

In a similar vein, 400 years ago Hamlet tells Laertes that he can rant as much as he likes, but Hamlet's time will come:

Hear you, sir,
What is the reason that you use me thus?
I loved you ever. But it is no matter.
Let Hercules himself do what he may,
The cat will mew, and dog will have his day.

But 'every dog has its day' is not just about revenge; it can also describe how humble people can also have their time in the sun. In *Don Quixote*, Cervantes describes how the Don and his squire are resting when they hear the pounding of hammers nearby. Sancho, the squire, is frightened and seeks to distract Don Knight from investigating this loud noise. So he spins a yarn about a goatherd whose overtures are spurned by the shepherdess Toralva,

Thereupon being grievous in the dumps about it, and now bitterly hating her, he e'en resolved to leave that country to get out of her sight: for now, as every dog has his day, the wench perceiving he came no longer a suitoring to her, but rather tossed his nose at her, and shunned her, she began to love him and dote upon him like any thing.

Perhaps the most widely-used example of this interpretation of the idiom in recent years was the remark Andy Warhol in 1968, 'in the future everybody will be world famous for fifteen minutes.'

SO WHO IS IT THAT HAD HIS DAY?

So much for the literary meanings of the idiom. I prefer its use to describe an exotic story of crazed affluence of an Indian royal in the 19th century. My dog story sprung out at me while I was on another mission—exploring the circumstances of my birth in India, two weeks after Indian independence in 1947. I learned how before India became a British colony in 1858, large parts of the country had been ruled by a private company, the East India Company which arrived in India in 1757. At its peak the East India Company had a private army three times the size of the British army.

My parents had lived in Rajasthan for 14 years where my father was in charge of a major hospital. My brother—seven years older—remembers living in a huge mansion and my mother having a pet baby elephant that came in the house. In fact I have a grainy film of the baby elephant's horrific capture in a sunken elephant trap. The elephant then had a servant dedicated to following it through the house to scoop up its poop.

Independence was marked by horrific violence. Riots between Hindus, Muslims and Sikhs spiralled out of control and trains carrying Hindus east to the new India and Muslims west to Pakistan, were torched. This resulted in some of the most brutal ethnic cleansing in modern history in which more than one million people were murdered. My mother was pregnant with me and my family wanted out. I was indeed a 'midnight's child' but not the kind Salman Rushdie wrote about in his famous novel. I was not a Hindu or a Muslim but a Brit who had no place now on the sub-continent but who insisted on hanging on to celebrate independence from colonial rule.

In seeking to understand these events around my birth, I was reading Midnight's Furies *by Nisid Hajari and was somewhat astounded by a dog story that sprung out as he chronicled the history:*

> *The state's Muslim nawab [Muslim ruling prince] was a vaguely ridiculous character, obsessed with dogs. His eight hundred canines supposedly each had their own apartment, complete with attendant and phone. A three-day 'wedding' between two favourites cost the state exchequer 3,000,000 rupees.*

Of course every dog has its day, but why didn't they have so many of their days between 1880 and 1960? And why did dog-weddings come back into fashion so dramatically after 1980? Perhaps weddings are not the only way in which dogs can have their day?

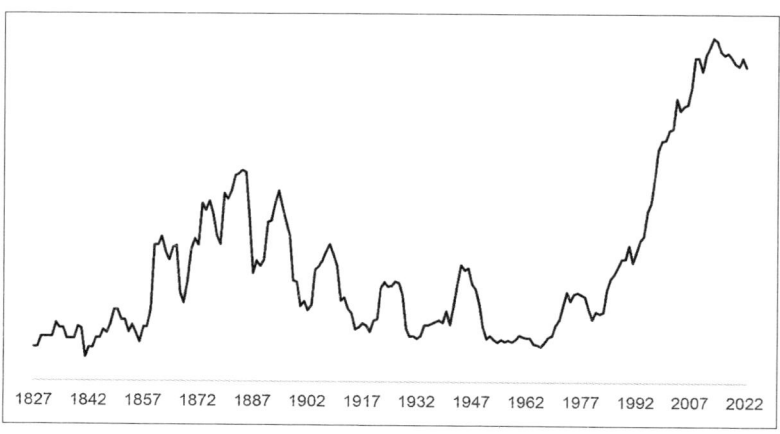

This Book is NOT

THE DOG'S BOLLOCKS

THE DOG'S BOLLOCKS refers to something which is excellent and 'outstanding'. But 'outstanding' has two slightly different meanings. The first, which is dominant nowadays, refers to a characteristic which is excellent, notably better than its rivals. The second and earlier meaning refers to a difference which is notable, not necessarily due to its excellence, but because it stands out.

The roots of this idiom can be traced back to the use of the word 'bollocks' in English slang. In the 18th century the word 'bollocks' referred to something which was 'nonsense' or 'rubbish'. In the early 20th century British street slang, 'bollocks' lost its exclusively negative meaning denoting 'nonsense' and also came to be used to represent difference, something which stands out from the average. Curiously, the first recording of its use was in 1937 in the typographical text :–. But it is not clear how this graphical representation developed, or what purpose it served.

During the 1980s, the interjection 'bollocks' morphed into the idiom 'the dog's bollocks', and came to be associated with excellence. Perhaps this was a result of its use in a 1986 musical performed in the Hampstead Theatre in London which used the phrase 'They are of the opinion that, when it comes to Italian opera, Pavarotti is the dog's bollocks.' Soon after *Viz*, a humorous magazine which described itself as being 'Not Suitable for Children, Old Farts or Guardians of Public Morals', entitled an issue in 1989 as *Viz—The Dog's Bollocks*. How it subsequently entered common parlance to denote excellence is not clear, but perhaps its vivid contrast to 'the cat's whiskers' is part of its attraction.

An almost certainly fictitious origin for this phrase was provided on the BBC's *IQ* TV programme which the programme's researchers must have enjoyed fabricating. Their fantasy takes us back to the 1930s and the Meccano construction sets, then very popular with children. The sets were produced the basic 'Box Standard' and the posher 'Box Deluxe' sizes. Over time, the phrase 'bog standard' came to signify something which was average, like the basic Meccano set. Supposedly, the workers assembling the posh Deluxe version began to refer to these sets as 'BD boxes', which then morphed to 'BD', from whence an easy jump to Dog's Bollocks. Really...? Stephen Fry, seemed a little sceptical of this elaborate story concocted by his researchers and closed the discussion of this 'true fact' with the phrase 'or so they say'.

The Dog's Bollocks

I first came across this rather colourful phrase during the second to last year of my six-year incarceration in a select single-sex English girls boarding school. The establishment was situated deep in the heart of rural nowhere, about 17 miles from the nearest train station, three miles from the

This Book is NOT

nearest retail outlet in the form of a tiny garage shop, and two and a half miles from the nearest all boys equivalent (but that is a story for another day).

I have often wondered what incredible foolhardiness or grim desperation would make any man opt to teach at a school like ours, but surprisingly there were a few brave souls that ventured into the particular St Trinian's Circle of Hell reserved for such hubris.

For some girls 'beefing' it up and down the La X [Lacrosse] pitches was sufficient; others took up smoking or drinking, and flirted with the odd eating disorder. In general however, the violent energy of raging synchronized hormones, boredom and teenage dissatisfaction would build in dorms and common rooms, corridors and practice rooms, spurting out in scalding jets of cruelty and sarcasm upon anyone unfortunate enough to come within range. It was indeed the perfect preparation for marriage, going to sleep and waking up next to someone you hated or who hated you. There were, however, some areas of unilateral bonding, and the general persecution and occasional lionization of male teachers was one such.

We delighted in inventing the most lurid fantasies and salacious rumours we could think of about them, mostly derived from a literary diet of Jilly Cooper, Emmanuele and Dennis Wheatley. We tormented the hapless Latin master, or 'Clammy Willie' as we called him, at every opportunity. The form room-blocks were freezing sheds where the majority of us had lessons, till we reached the carpet tiled luxury of the sixth form. It faced on to fields full of cheerfully randy Friesian bullocks and our wide eyed question 'Mr …, What are those cows DOING?' was met with a terse 'turn to page 11' in Approach to Latin. The dark flush over his cheeks was all we gleefully desired. Occasionally in the summer, we would slowly begin every five minutes to undress, button by button, complaining how hot it was. Till once more flushed and furious he demanded we stop this ridiculous behaviour immediately. We fell about in fits of giggles knowing we had swimming straight after and all had our costumes on underneath.

There was one member of staff who had been a major in the war and counted in Malay and gave you toffees if you got the answer correct. We loved him 'such an old teddy bear.' On him we lavished the genuine affection that we couldn't or wouldn't show our absent fathers.

I come now to the two males that almost the entire school had crushes on, plus the one whom this story primarily concerns. The first, known as the BSM, was the building site manager working on the construction of the new Art Block. I hope he secretly enjoyed our slavish attentions and dismissed us as the silly naïve girls that we were, despite our imagined sophistication and knowing airs; few of us had so much as snogged a boy, let alone had sex.

In an unusual swerve towards modernism, the choir mistress, Norky Boobs, herself a cautionary tale being what you got if you wore an inadequate bra, was replaced by a young and surprisingly handsome man. This rather ambitious new choir master had obviously been lured by the fact that it was a musical school, of high Anglican persuasion, with a lot of choral singing and which boasted a large chapel with an organ. Well aware of his universal 'dishiness' he rashly pulled out all the stops and subsequently had to leave under a cloud, having made a member of the Senior Choir pregnant. Quel scandal!

From a young man who clearly 'thought' he was the dog's bollocks, we now turn to the male who truly WAS. Madam Wardress as our head mistress was officially titled, the keeper of the keys, had a familiar, in the shape of a rust coloured Hungarian Vizsla dog by the name of Guardian. If he could talk, he would probably have sounded like Lesley Phillips in full 'Ding Dong' mode. He was very 'over sexed' and would unfailingly attempt to mount the leg of anybody who stood still long enough. We of course alleged that he and his mistress were way more than friends, but that was the way our tragic little febrile minds worked.

One day whilst crossing from the Junior Library through the front hall, where we were not supposed to linger, I stood in rapt amazement. That American oddity Maggie Finklestein from the Upper Fifth was standing with her parents who had come to take her for a 'Special Exeat'

Mrs Gloria Finklestein, had clearly decided to dress in her interpretation of a lady from The County Life Magazine, *resplendent in canary yellow tweed, a huge mink coat, and shock horror! quantities of diamonds worn before lunch. Bracelets jangling, in a whirl of enthusiasm, she swept towards Madam Wardress's reception room exclaiming over the delightful portraits, plasterwork etc. as she proceeded. Here she encountered Guardian at his most welcoming...*

If the idiom really did originate in a Meccano factory in the 1930s, it appears that none of the workforce bothered to write about their packing proclivities! It is also possible that the word 'bollocks' was too salacious for literary conversation until the 1980s. But at least the Hampstead Theatre (or was it Pavarotti or even – shock horror – *Viz*) which freed the shackles of polite conversation and allowed the idiom to flourish. Whatever the case, we seem to have got become bored with our freedom to talk about naughty bits in recent years.

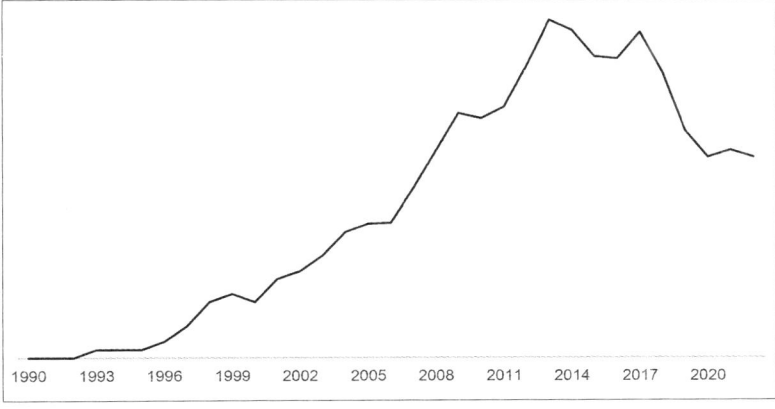

YOU CAN'T TEACH AN OLD DOG
NEW TRICKS

THE MEANING of this idiom is self-evident—the older you are the less your capacity to learn new things. The origins of this idiom in the English language can be traced back to John Fitzherbert, the author of *The boke of hvsbandry*, published in 1534. This was a piece of literal advice offered to those training their sheep dogs—'The dogge must lerne it, whan he is a whelpe, or els it wyl not be: for it is harde to make an olde dogge to stoupe.'

Two centuries later this practical admonition to sheep herders had entered the English language as an idiom. Nathan Bradley's collection of *Divers Proverbs* published in 1721 traces the roots of this English idiom to ancient Greece and Rome.

It may or may not be true that older people (and dogs) find it harder to learn new ideas. Some scientists believe that with the exception of learning new languages, older people are just as able to take in new concepts and change their behaviour as their younger counterparts. The problem is that their 'hard discs' (brain stores) are full with accumulated trash and they have had more years to develop habits which are no longer appropriate in an era of rapid change. To make matters worse, we are experiencing a wave of exceptionally rapid and radical technological changes, driven primarily by advances in electronics. These affect not just the physical instruments which we use (the internet and smart phones rather than fixed lines and the post) but the way we interact with each other. Unlike younger people who were 'born electronic', older and disadvantaged people have a major knowledge mountain to climb in the face of these new challenges. So its not that older people cannot learn, but rather that they have more to learn. This problem is particularly acute when old skills are superseded by new ones—we no longer repair devices, but need to master the internet to download what are fancifully called 'upgrades'.

But let's suppose that it is indeed the case that you can't teach an old dog new tricks. That raises a major problem in the way in which our societies are governed, since older leaders may be ill-equipped to cope with modern challenges. President Biden turned 80 during his term of office. His less-old challenger, 'dirty-dog-Donald-Trump' (although the description *challenger* doesn't really capture his chaotic, greedy, misogynistic character) won the election in 2024 at the youthful age of 79. And its not just in America that older leaders (mis)lead their countries. In 2024 more than one-third of executive heads of state were in their 60s, and five percent were in their 80s. Paul Biya was president of Cameroon for more than 40 years and (mis)led the country until he was over 90; Mahmoud Abbas was president of the West Bank of Palestine when he was 88; Ali Khamenei was the supreme leader of Iran for more than 30 years and was born in 1939, and Robert Mugabe was eventually forced out of office in Zimbabwe when he was 93. A ropey classification of so-called free countries (compiled by Freedom House) estimated that the median age of leaders in 'not-free' countries was 69, 61 in 'partly-free' countries and 58 in 'free' countries.

But don't diss older people who are unwilling or unable to learn new tricks. The thrusting techies who have given us the new tricks of social media are overwhelmingly young, and the harms caused by the misuse of social media are predominantly a result of the irresponsible and reprehensible behaviour of younger people. Maybe the problem lies more with the desire and capacity to adopt new tricks rather than the supposed incapacity of older generations to 'get with it'.

YOU CAN'T TEACH AN OLD DOG NEW TRICKS

Several years ago, with two friends in tow, I cycled from Burkino Faso to Timbuktu in Mali. To cross the border into Mali we cycled along sandy tracks, in blistering heat that sucked every cell of energy from our rattled bodies. At night, crumbling shacks and grimy stalls lurked in the shadows of countless fires. Even the vultures rummaging through heaps of rubbish looked dejected. We slept on the roofs of mud houses in the hope of snatching a cool breeze and the early mornings were broken by the **adhan**, *the call to prayer. The people were warm and welcoming and generous in spite of the little they had.*

It was a relief to continue pedalling northwards and to arrive in Ouahigouya where we were offered an audience with the **naba**, *the king of the Yatengo province. The* **naba** *presided over thirty wives and lived in a dilapidated but delightful mud compound built before French domination. His power was only surpassed by the* **naba** *of the capital, Ougadougou and he was revered by all. The government, we were told, would seek his consent in all matters.*

Following instructions to remove our battered, dusty trainers and not to stand up, we crawled through a gap in the hut on all fours. Before us sat the wise old gentleman on a rudimentary large wooden royal seat, flicking away the flies with the tail of an unidentifiable animal.

With the help of an interpreter, the **naba** *informed us in a growly, hushed voice that he was at least a hundred years old. A member of his entourage enquired as to what gifts we had brought him? Well prepared, we handed over a rolled gold wrist-watch and some costume jewellery in exchange for ancient wisdom. The three of us battered him with endless questions. Here was someone serving us our futures. He dished out imaginative predictions and we drank in every drop of it.*

I wonder if it was the crawling towards the 'king' on all fours, his craggy, saggy face, and the orders not to interrupt him and under no circumstances to turn our backs on departure, that led us to sit enraptured at his feet, mouths agape. These were not pearls that fell from his toothless mouth but diamond studded jewels.

The population of Burkino Faso, once able to choose their religion (Christian, Muslim or animist) and once free to choose their colourful mode of dress, is now forced to wear burqas and is under the yoke of Islamist armed groups allied with Al-Qaeda and the Islamic State (Isis)

Yet I believe that no-one is going to teach that old dog, the **naba**, *new tricks. Hopefully he is still reigning over his Kingdom of Yatengo, now in his bicentennial year.*

Angie Butler, Jill of All Trades, Mistress of None (except my dog)
Oxfordshire, UK.

This Book is NOT

It looks like an increasing number of people found it easy to learn new tricks during the second half of the 20th century. But what went wrong after that? Was it the introduction of the internet and the smart phone which flummoxed us?

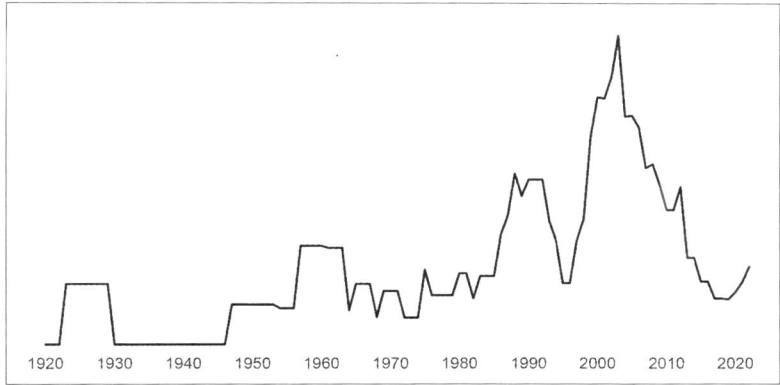

This Book is NOT

DOGGING

WHILST THE idiom 'to dog' has a long history describing pestering and 'dogged' behaviour, the modern use of the idiom 'dogging' refers to the practice of having sex in a public space with the expressed aim of allowing the public to watch, and in some cases even to join-in. Usually, dogging occurs in cars in public car parks. In England dogging is not illegal.

The use of public venues for sex was first mentioned in 1853. The organised and 'open' practice of dogging in cars has increased since the 1970s and has been facilitated by the introduction of the internet and mobile phones (is this why they are called 'smartphones'?). There are now also an increasing number of dogging WhatsApp communities.

Historically, dogging appears to be a peculiarly British practice, or more specifically an English 'hobby'. Its popularity spread from northern England, and particularly Manchester which it is said to be the capital of dogging in the UK. (Why dogging was popularised in the North is beyond comprehension. However since no one has done a thorough survey of English doggers, it may not even be true!) Whatever its origins and geographical concentration, dogging is on the increase. A survey of 260 English country parks in the early 2000s found that 60 per cent had seen an increase in dogging. Another survey in 2021 identified and listed more than 60 dogging locations in Essex (in the South of England) alone. Some swinging sex groups even have cars in their nightclubs and in one case, a truck-cab to allow a larger number of doggers to participate!

The days of English soft-power are not over and dogging has begun to spread to other countries, not least to neighbouring Ireland. Our poor American cousins don't get it though, since in American slang dogging refers to lazy sports people who don't exert themselves in the game. What are they missing?

There are no established explanations why this form of 'sport' is called dogging. Perhaps, as some speculate, it is because dog-walkers stumbled upon people having casual sex in the open. Even if this is true, how does that include the practice of inviting strangers to join in? Another explanation is that voyeurs would patrol beauty spots and relentlessly 'dog' (spy on) couples seeking rural solitude to spice up their sex lives. Or perhaps it may also follow from the excuse given to surprised outdoor lovers that they were 'just walking their dogs'.

THE RULES OF DOGGING

Like all 'sport', even informal sports, dogging has its own rules. So here are some advisories if you want to join the throng. If you want someone to watch you, park in the open space, then flash your headlights or leave the lights on. If you want someone to join you, leave the door open. And if you want oral sex, open your window halfway (what...?). And as Carley Odell reported in the Leicester Mercury, *good doggers need to have manners, so here is her list of 14 etiquette rules*

1 *Wear a condom, to prevent any Sexually Transmitted Diseases or unwanted pregnancies. It is even advised to take a box of condoms to share around with fellow doggers.*
2 *Do not 'dog' in front of children or unsuspecting passers-by.*
3 *Refrain from disturbing the peace or attracting attention.*
4 *Anonymity is key. No one should reveal the identity of other doggers and you should create a dogging name to protect your identity.*
5 *Do not destroy public property or trespass on private property.*
6 *All condoms and rubbish should be collected and discarded in a bin.*
7 *Legal driving and parking should always be practised.*
8 *Agree a signal or safe word in case one of the you wants to stop.*
9 *It is not generally accepted for a woman to turn up to a dogging location alone. It is advised that she takes a man she trusts with her to protect her interests.*
10 *Steer clear of areas known for prostitution and drug dealing.*
11 *If watching, you should not touch unless verbally invited to do so.*
12 *If you're willing for people to watch, flash your interior light. If you want watchers to come closer or join in, roll down your window.*
13 *Don't leave headlights on once you have arrived at the scene.*

14   *When finished, drive around for a while or stop for food to make sure you're not being followed.*

Dogging is not always a comfortable experience. One frequent female dogger complained that when it's cold, not all men can perform effectively. She also reported that she was once forced to make a rapid exit when the entrant to her car was not a man (as she expected and hoped) but a fox (surely not a vixen?).

Raphie Kaplinsky,
Development Economist (Retired)
Barcombe Mills, UK.

We will probably never know why dogging fell out of favour during the second half of the 20th century. But thank goodness the practice seems to have revived in recent years. How else could we satisfy our salacious greed? Perhaps its recent popularity is due to the introduction of the internet and social media? But if so, how did the word spread in the nineteenth century? So many unknowns about such a crucial topic...

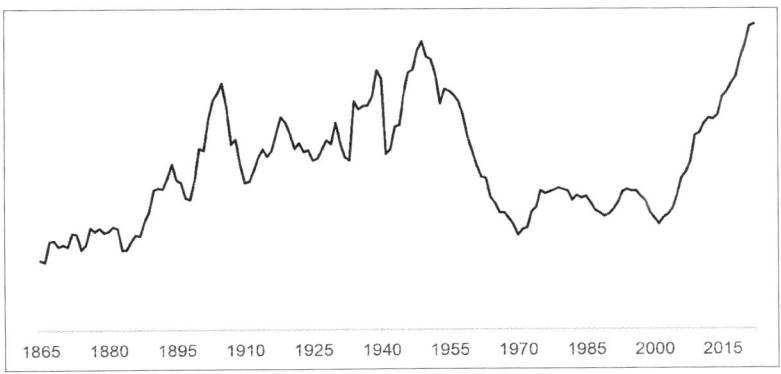

DOGS CAN SPEAK, BUT ONLY TO THOSE WHO KNOW HOW TO LISTEN

THIS recent idiom was introduced by the Turkish Nobel Literature Laureate Orhan Pamuk in his book *My Name is Red*, published in 1998 and then translated into English in 2001. The meaning of the idiom is self-evident—unless you are emotionally attuned to someone (including a dog) you will not be able to understand what they are really saying. Pamuk writes: 'I'm a dog, and because you humans are much less rational beasts than I, you're telling yourselves 'Dogs don't talk'... Dogs do speak, but only to those who know how to listen'. One of the central characters in the book is Shekure (the name is derived from the word 'sugar' and also happens to be the name of Pamuk's mother) who observes 'just like those beautiful women with one eye on the life within the book and one eye on the life outside, I, too, long to speak with you who are observing me from who knows which distant time and place.'

POPPY SPOKE AND WE HEARD

My story of Poppy illustrates that it is not just humans who need to listen to their dogs (dead or alive), but other dogs too.

Poppy was found wandering, one day late in 2004, on a long-abandoned railway crossing in the centre of Addis Ababa in Ethiopia and would have surely fallen under the wheels of a passing car, had I not rescued her. I had recently moved into an old house with a large garden and Poppy became part of an extended family, joining us for long walks at the weekend in Entoto, the hills surrounding Addis.

All was good until the day in late 2006 when I was posted to Latin America. Santiago, Chile was a long way away, and it seemed too much to put the dog through a plane journey that would have lasted a day and a half, with a long wait-over in Europe. Moreover, Santiago was a city of high-rise apartments—long walks would be a distant dream.

This Book is NOT

So I left Poppy behind with much guilt, and a broken heart. Sadly, Poppy was neglected by the family I had left her with and was attacked (well, raped) by other dogs. My former housekeeper Dagma visited her and was shocked and angry to see the dog half-staved, injured and clearly in distress. She moved Poppy to an old friend of mine, Zahra.

Zahra was Muslim from Djibouti, and Muslims often don't appreciate close proximity to dogs. But she cared wonderfully for Poppy. Whenever I was back in Addis, I visited Zahra—Poppy somehow always knew I was coming before I even approached the gate of the house. However, eventually Zahra also had to move for professional reasons. So Poppy was again homeless, until, through some convoluted connections, she ended up in the house of the charge d'affaire of the Serbian embassy who doted on the good-natured Poppy. My visits became increasingly infrequent.

And then, the opportunity came for a long-wished-for reposting in Africa! Not Ethiopia this time, but Rwanda, 2,500 kms from Addis. Two years later the Serbian couple found themselves finishing their tour of duty, and Poppy was potentially homeless once again. The solution was clear—Poppy needed to come to Rwanda and to live with me, after eight years of separation (which, remember, for a dog, is over half a century). There was just one problem—by then I had gained another dog, a stray whom I called Bakame (Big Eared Rabbit in Kinyarwanda). And I wasn't sure they were going to get along.

Poppy had a traumatic air journey from Addis to Kigali and arrived anxious and barking. But as soon as she heard my voice she calmed down. I took her home from the airport and she rushed out to explore the backyard, only to find another dog in the garden! Despite the occasional tension between the two dogs, they got on well and life was blissful. Well, almost blissful, because Bakame irritated Poppy by constantly smelling her backside. I mistakenly thought it was a dog obsession with backsides and the fact that Poppy had had some problems of internal bleeding ever since she had been gang-raped back in Addis.

However, Poppy's problem was more serious. She had started hiding under the bushes sometimes and growling aggressively. Bakame sensed something that I could not know, but dogs can, because they are able to smell and sense disease. It took me time to really listen to Poppy's pain and I eventually took her to one of the few Rwandan vets in a country which at the time only had 600 doctors. I looked into Poppy's eyes and caressed her; she wagged her tail and I left her with the vet for treatment. I hadn't got far down the road when I received a phone call to return. Alfonse broke the bad news—Poppy had a large inoperable tumour and her pain would only get worse. I felt sick—only the year before, I had spent nine months battling a lymphoma which nearly cost me my own life. I caressed Poppy as she was anaesthetised. Poppy jolted violently, protesting that her life was being taken away from her. I felt I had betrayed her and struggled hard not to vomit.

On arriving home, Bakame was waiting eagerly. But as the boot of the car was opened, she immediately sensed something was wrong. She jumped up into the car and could not understand why Poppy would not move. She was distressed and had to be pulled away from Poppy and put in a room at the back of the house. I asked Tantine, my gardener, to assist with the burial. She was initially reticent—I was told that in Rwandan culture it is bad luck to touch the body of a dead person or animal, and she would have to perform a special rite to free herself of the bad karma. Tantine spoke no French nor English, so I had to ask Elisabeth, the cleaner, to convince her to assist (a financial reward seemed to make a difference).

Poppy was not a large dog. We wrapped her in a cloth and buried her in a shallow grave. I let Bakame out of the room, and went to lie down, feeling unwell, with the sensation I had somehow betrayed Poppy. About 30 minutes later there was a cry from the terrace of the house. I rushed out—what was the problem? The gardener pointed … Poppy was lying on the ground in the middle of the garden! My heart raced—she was not dead? Had she somehow still miraculously survived? Had we buried her while she was still breathing? Tantine, Elisabeth and Jacques (the house-guard) did not want to approach, and looked horrified, and not a little bit scared: what was this magic that had resurrected the dog from its grave?

My first thought was that, by some crazy chance, Poppy was still breathing and alive. Perhaps, after all, I would have the opportunity to say a proper goodbye. But I quickly realised that she was not breathing and was still lifeless. I looked around—how this had happened?

This Book is NOT

> *Then the penny dropped. I found Bakame on the other side of the house, sitting in a corner, looking sheepish. I looked down at her paws—they were covered in dirt. Poppy may not have been best friend but as she had clearly told Bakame she did not belong in the ground! The indignity of it!*
>
> *The final task was to find a fitting resting place for Poppy, out of Bakame's reach. At the back of the house, there was a stone terrace, perhaps ten feet high, with a small slither of garden on the top. It seemed to be the perfect place...so we lifted the dead dog on a wooden ladder and dug a hole on top of the terrace, overlooking the house. The gardener planted a bush in the place where Poppy was buried, and it flourishes to this day. She still talks to me and I do listen...*
>
> *Andy Mold, Economist,*
> *Economic Commission for Africa*
> *Kigali, Rwanda.*

Dogs spoke to us during the roaring 20s and the great depression and then before the great financial crisis in 2008? Did we listen? Probably not, since they seem to have stopped bothering over the past decade.

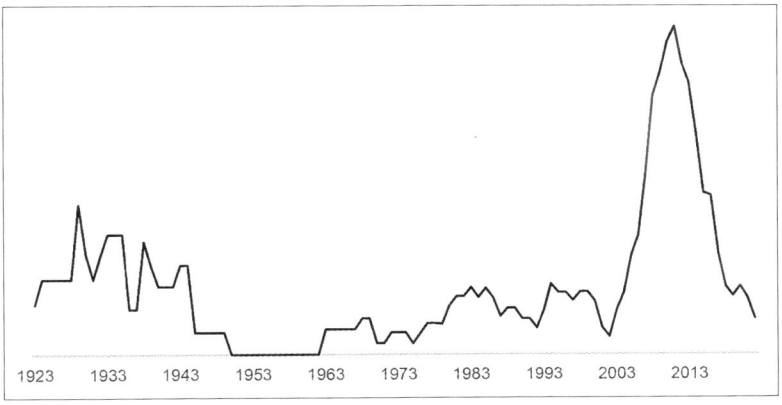

RAINING CATS AND DOGS

THIS IDIOM is used to describe very heavy, torrential, rain. Disappointingly, although there are records of smaller creatures such as frogs, fish and spiders being sucked up by water spouts from ponds and raining down on earth, the bad news is that dogs and cats do not seem to have been included. Nor for that matter have giraffes and elephants rained down in storms.

This idiom originated in graphical representations of the Norse god of storms, Odin, which frequently included dogs and black cats (who rode rain-storms on broomsticks) to symbolise wind. In ancient Greek, the Greek word 'κατάδουποι' (sometimes 'cata doxa', cats dogs) was used to describe unbelievable experiences, originating from the word used to describe the turmoil of rapids on the Nile. Latin, ancient French and English all used the word 'catadupe', literally meaning waterfall, to characterise turmoil.

No one seems to believe the myth that the idiom refers to cats and dogs being swept into houses from their refuge in rain-sodden thatched roofs (since amongst other things, thatched roofs are water-proof). Perhaps this myth was fostered by the imagery in Jonathan Swift's 1710 poem *Description of a City Shower*—'Drowned puppies, stinking sprats, all drenched in mud, Dead cats and turnip-tops come tumbling down the flood'. But Swift's poem was not the first in English to use this image: Henry Vaughan's poem in 1651 used the image of a roof which was secure against 'dogs and cats rained in shower' and in 1652 Richard Brome's *City Witt* included the line 'It shall rain dogs and polecats'.

I AM STILL WAITING FOR THE CATS AND DOGS

Glastonbury, the behemoth festival, takes place in mid-summer and offers something (and often many things) for everyone—performing arts, music, theatre, comedy, madness and fun. In 1997 it excelled in its generosity, offering not just entertainment but also a free load of mud, rain, thunder, lightning, mud, mud and mud. The deluge was historic and the wettest ever recorded—it turned the famous dairy farm into a complete bog. I was there and can confirm that it rained cats and dogs from the day it began to the day it ended.

I was excited as I had recently qualified as a 'shiatsu practitioner'. Now was my opportunity to offer some payback—free shiatsu treatments in the festival's 'chill-out healing fields'. Revellers could enjoy the serenity of being healed in a magical atmosphere. I was thrilled to have an oppor-tunity to share my new-found skills with my love of music. There were limitless crowds and I had to push my way through, carrying my heavy knapsack, tent, blow-up mattress, water bottle and festival necessities. I felt truly well prepared. Little did I know…

Taking time to find my own space and to erect my minuscule tent amongst my fellow shiatsu practitioners, I contentedly lay on my back listening to the sound of healing gongs, chanting and drumming.

Gazing up at the sky I noticed a dark shroud covering the magical glow on the rolling green fields dotted with colourful tents. Mmmm… ominous… dramatic weather event? Surely not—its mid-summer! It was then a huge shock when the heavy rains thundered down on the world's biggest music festival.

The immense volume of water rapidly soaked the dry, dusty earth and in no time turned vast areas of the festival into giant pools of soupy brown liquid, up to a foot deep. However, as in all grand events, the show carried on. Then, in the evening, after treating exhausted, sodden and confused folk with compassion and warmth, we gathered around the camp-fire, covering ourselves in whatever we could find and also bandaging our shoes in black plastic bags.

There was an amazing line up of musicians playing that year—so the herculean effort of leaving our warm fire to attend the events was worth it. We chose the closest venues and made our way through the sludge to the nearest World Jazz stage. There we listened to brilliant musicians such as Nitin Sawhney, Afro- Celt, Cheikh Lo and David Byrne.

But what a struggle to keep myself organised with my tent sinking into the mud. It was important to ensure that my boots, torch, loo paper and water bottle were all close to hand. I needed to make my way through the sludge to the long-drop loos. Once I arrived, I discovered they were to be avoided—a horror beyond all horrors. There was no alternative. I was forced to pee in my biscuit tin—the biscuits having been decanted before rather than after relieving myself.

After the questionable relief at finding the long-drop loos I set out to explore the many 'world cuisine' food stalls. I was proud I had managed to acquire a portable stool so I could sit and enjoy the food. However this was little comfort as it was virtually impossible to sit without sinking into inches of sludge.

This was the first year that the festival organisers had erected solar heated showers. However, since the cats and dogs had blocked out the warming sun, showering required too much fortitude. Instead we stripped down to our naked muddy bodies and ran under a hosepipe hanging off

This Book is NOT

a branch. Someone then came up with the bright idea of using a sewage gulper to suck up the mud on the slippery dance tent. Great idea but he set it on 'blow' rather than 'suck'… and the mud scattered everywhere!

It took me over an hour trudging past queues of people knee-deep in mud to get to the grand finale at the pyramid stage where Radiohead performed. The light show illuminated the shining mud and the dark, sodden clouds. But despite my best efforts I was unable to catch sight of any cats and dogs left behind by the showers. Never mind—there was an amazing sense of unity and acceptance as we embraced the shared experience.

The 1997 Glastonbury festival is renowned as an historic event of music, madness and mud. Yes, it was indeed truly wonderful, memorable, extraordinary and unforgettable. But I have no desire to repeat the experience even if a future deluge would serve up a treat of cats and dogs.

Tikki Kyte, Shiatsu Practitioner (Retired)
Andalucia, Spain.

Perhaps the recent rise in references to 'cats and dogs' reflects the onset of climate change? Hands up those who have actually seen it raining cats and dogs.

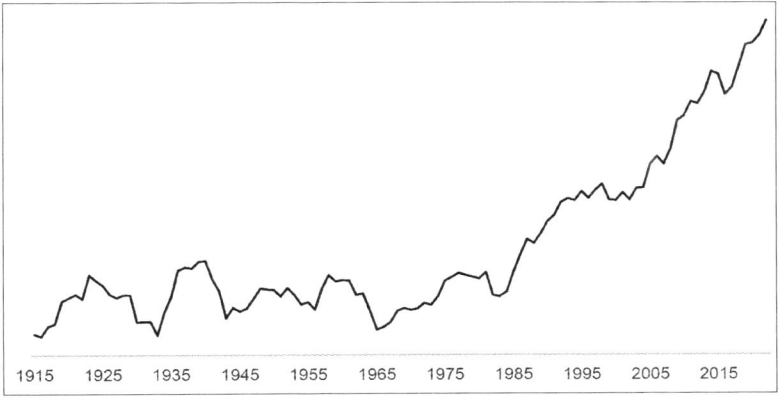

THE FACTORY OF THE FUTURE
WILL HAVE ONLY TWO EMPLOYEES,
A MAN AND A DOG
The human will feed the dog and the dog will make
sure that no one touches the machinery

THIS IDIOM has two related meanings. First, it warns us about the power of technology to destroy jobs, a challenge which is now particularly acute in the age of Artificial Intelligence and robots. And, second, with tongue in cheek, the idiom parodies the 'superior intelligence' of automated machinery in the face of limited human capabilities.

This is a relatively recent aphorism which is often mistakenly attributed to Warren Bennis, an American professor of business management. Bennis drew on the idiom in 1989, but made it clear that it was not his creation. Instead, it seems that it originated with a remark by a British trade unionist during the 1970s reflecting on the potential of the new System X electronic telephone exchange to destroy jobs. His remark was picked up by an Australian newspaper (*The Age*, in Melbourne) and by the *Guardian* newspaper in the UK in 1983, and in *Datamation*, an industry trade journal in 1987.

Concern with the job destroying power of new technology is not new. After the 1730s there was a wave of mechanisation in the English textile industry. The first machines mechanising cotton spinning reduced the price of cotton thread by fifteen times. But at the same time as reducing costs, the machinery swept aside the jobs of highly-paid skilled workers. This led to a wave of machine-breaking by workers in the textile industry who feared for their livelihoods. Calling themselves after an apocryphal apprentice Ned Ludd who was said to have destroyed knitting machines, in 1811-1812 a group of 'Luddite' workers set out to destroy the new machinery—'Plunder is not our object, the common necessaries of life is what we at present aim at'. Since then the resistance to job-displacing innovation in order to protect jobs is referred to as Luddism.

This heartfelt cry by the affected workers was to no avail and the

English parliament responded with laws imposing capital punishment for machine-breaking (a step-up in severity from the previous policy of deportation to Australia). The poet Lord Byron spoke out eloquently and sarcastically in parliament against this draconian response:

> In the foolishness of their hearts, they [the workers destroying machinery] imagined that the maintenance and well doing of the industrious poor, were objects of greater consequence than the enrichment of a few individuals by any improvement in the implements of trade which threw the workmen out of employment, and rendered the labourer unworthy of his hire.

Referring to the impoverishment of displaced workers, Byron continued:

> I have traversed the seat of war in the peninsula; I have been in some of the most oppressed provinces of Turkey; but never, under the most despotic of infidel governments, did I behold such squalid wretchedness as I have seen since my return, in the very heart of a Christian country.

The industrialising world has witnessed many eras of job-destroying technological innovation since the mechanisation of cotton spinning machinery in 19th century England. But, in each phase, whilst many people saw their skills and wages devalued and their jobs destroyed, new forms of employment were created. For example, between the end of the Second World War and the end of the golden age economic boom in the early 1970s, the numbers employed in (relatively high wage) manufacturing in the US increased only marginally from 17 million to 19 million workers. But in the same period the numbers employed in (generally less-well paid) services, construction, transport and finance more than doubled from 19 million to almost 40 million.

With the advance of artificial intelligence and robots, once again we need to grapple with the challenges created by job-destroying technological change. But this time it is not the wages and work of skilled manual workers which are threatened, but the welfare of the highly skilled. From the 1980s, the livelihoods of many highly skilled industrial workers in the rich countries were undermined by the use of cheap manual labour in the developing world. This challenge to living standards in the rich countries extended to many skilled workers in the first two decades of the 21st century—legal contracts were being scanned by Indian lawyers, and X-rays being read by radiologists in South Africa. But now with the advance of AI, the livelihoods of skilled workers are being threatened every-where, in rich and poor countries alike. As one observer remarked, automation is now blind to the colour of your collar.

As in all previous eras when radical new technologies have been introduced, there are both winners and losers. There will be winners as AI diffuses. A recent study by the Organisation of Economic Cooperation and Development concluded that the rapid advance of AI and robots offers the scope for improved productivity, for new products (for example, major advances in pharmaceuticals), a reduction in the tedium of work and greater safety in work. It also offers job-creating opportunities for employment (especially young and educated workers) trained in new AI-related skills. But at the same time it threatens future livelihoods of many highly skilled workers, likely to have big social and political consequences.

BEWARE OF ADVANCED AUTOMATION

But don't believe all the hype. Here are two cautionary tales to keep you awake.

The first concerns the crashes of two Boeing 737 Max aircraft. This is one of the most advanced aeroplanes developed over the past two decades. It was designed to be really clever, with many automated controls prevent-ing pilot error. And in many respects it is a very clever aeroplane, making for smoother flights, reducing the need for aircrew and saving fuel. Except that it had a design error in a tiny sensor measuring its altitude. The

This Book is NOT

sensor gave the plane incorrect instructions, the planes began to behave erratically and to descend suddenly. The two pilots tried 21 times to override the automated system (no dog was guarding their controls!), but the 'clever' automated system would not allow them to act appropriately. 346 people were killed in two crashes, one in Indonesia and the other in Ethiopia.

If that example doesn't keep you awake at night, try this one. The weaponry in modern warfare is becoming increasingly sophisticated, and automation and AI is making it more so. An 'operator' sitting in front of a computer screen in Nevada, Milton Keynes or Jerusalem can unleash an unmanned drone to wreak destruction on an isolated rural household in virtually any part of the world without the 'handlers' (what a curious phrase for an automated killing system) having any physical exposure to the devastation their systems are unleashing. This 'clever automation' is already reality. But we are now moving to a world in which the decision to unleash weaponry will not be made by an interfering human but by an 'intelligent' (what….?) weapon system without any reference to a human input. The weaponry will assess the complex situation and using inferential learning, will make decisions independent of human control. Gruesome? Yes. But what if the weaponry is really devastating (perhaps even a nuclear bomb) and what if this 'intelligent, inferential learning' weaponry system is so clever that it pays no attention to orders from its human-minders to desist? And in some scary science-fiction scenarios, the weaponry sees itself as being threatened by its human minder, turns on its self- preservation mode and focuses its destructive force directly on its controller who it perceives to have 'gone rogue'.

So, contrary to the idiom's intent, lets not invent a factory where the human is unable to control the machinery, and for goodness sake, get rid of the dog!

Raphie Kaplinsky, Development Economist (Retired)
Barcombe Mills, UK.

IN THE DOGHOUSE

THE IDIOM being *sent to the doghouse* describes a form of temporary rebuke. Your behaviour has fallen down in some way, and as a consequence you will be excluded from a relationship, or perhaps a marital bed, in the expectation that you will not repeat the transgression. In general the idiom refers to exclusion from an intimate relationship, although it can also describe a minor sanction due to bad behaviour in a working environment. But don't worry—in time you will be readmitted. As in the case of a dog which is temporarily banished to its kennel due to its bad behaviour, there is a playful element to this idiom. A closely related idiom describes an errant partner (usually the husband) arriving home much later than expected to find a scrawled note on the kitchen table 'welcome home; your food is in the dog'.

There is some dispute about the origin of this idiom. Some believe that it can be traced back to J M Barrie's *Peter Pan* written in 1911. The family dog Nana lived in an outdoor doghouse. When the remorseful father blames himself for the kidnapping of his children by Captain Hook, he goes to the doghouse in penitence.

> Having thought the matter out with anxious care after the flight of the children, he went down on all fours and crawled into the kennel. To all Mrs. Darling's dear invitations to him to come out he replied sadly but firmly: 'No, my own one, this is the place for me.'

But this origin is disputed on the basis that Barrie lived in Scotland where dogs lived in kennels and not doghouses. Instead, a doghouse is said to be a quintessential American phrase and the well-known chronicler of idioms, Gary Martin (www.phrases.org. uk), believes that that it was first used in print in a 1926 glossary of terms describing criminal behaviour written by Finerty, the commissioner of police in Bessemer, Pennsylvania.

However, it is also possible that the idiom of being put into a doghouse as a temporary measure of discomfort can be traced back to the slave trade or the Crimean War during the mid-nineteenth century. The ship's crew were forced to sleep in kennel-style structures on the hot and humid decks for some or most of the journey's duration. Eventually the journey came to an end, and they were released into more salubrious accommodation. In a memoir of his travels, in 1840 James Holman described this shipboard accommodation as comprising 'a doghouse (a box about six feet long, four high, and two broad) containing a mattress fitted about 18 inches from the deck'. In this derivation there is no sense of temporary punishment for bad behaviour, least of all with a playful element, which is what this idiom is about, so this is an unlikely source of the idiom's origin.

THE DOG AND THE PSYCHE

Jason doesn't like dogs so when Marianne suggested getting a cocka-poo, he was set against it. Marianne and their children thought that a dog would be a positive addition to their family. In due course a puppy came to live with them. Jason was not interested in the dog but all thought that, eventually, he would be won over by the little character. Not so. Four years on he is indifferent to the dog. He has no relationship with it; but he is the one it obeys; if he orders it to come in from the garden it does so immediately. The dog is in his family house but he is in the family's doghouse.

Today I went for a walk with my mini poodle. I was enjoying the sun and she was enjoying chasing sticks and running off the lead. There was an incident of very bad behaviour when she squeezed through the railings into a no-dog area of the park (I don't think she can read the signs in English). She ignored my command to desist and by the time I could get round the fence and through a gate to reach her she had eaten left over, unidentified food and the foil in which it was wrapped. She doesn't realise that there is a direct link between this behaviour and walks on the lead only! She is in the doghouse, but I will forgive her soon.

Pondering the difference between those who welcome dogs into their lives and those who don't, it emerged that there is possibly a psychological

This Book is NOT

reason why Jason is indifferent to his family dog. As a child Jason lived in South America. At the time, there were street dogs who were a danger to people as they carried rabies and travelled in packs. When he was five years old, he was bitten by one of these dogs, which was a very frightening experience. One can imagine his parents' concern at the time. Being bitten would be a traumatic experience for a small child but, as well, the worry about the danger of rabies would have contributed to the concern of the adults around him. So Jason grew up with a justified fear of, and disdain for, these animals. The young Jason and his family no doubt wished that all of the dogs would be kept in doghouses.

There is a psychological reason why, unlike Jason, I always have a dog in my life. As a child my mother used to tell of how, aged three, she had fallen in the river Thames at Maidenhead and had been rescued from drowning by her boxer dog, who dragged her to safety. When I was a child, living in Sussex, I had a large standard poodle. He came into my life when I was four and died when I was 16. Peter Pan was my favourite childhood story; I read and reread it, was taken to see it performed on the stage in London, and my sister and I enacted it, playing all the parts. This was long before it was given the Disney animation treatment. Nana, the St Bernard dog, is an important character in Peter Pan; she is nursemaid to the children and their protector. It is when she is locked in a kennel and the children are left unguarded, that the children fly away, with Peter Pan, to the Never Land. The father banishes himself to the doghouse (kennel) in remorse for keeping the dog kennelled. So Nana, was a guardian and our dog was given that role too. As quite small children my sister and I used to roam the South Downs with our friends. We were aware of the danger posed by strangers and our parents were insistent that we took our dog with us. Moreover if I was scared at night the dog was allowed to sleep in my room so that I felt safe. So I was raised seeing the dog as a protector and a companion. Our dog lived in our house unlike Nana who lived in the doghouse.

Perhaps these examples offer a little understanding of some of the psychological differences between those who welcome the dog into their house, and those who are in the doghouse for not doing so.

Joy Schaverien, Jungian Analyst
London, UK

The spike in references in the mid-20th century suggests that perhaps the origin of this idiom really was a way of describing criminal behaviour rather than Barrie's *Peter Pan* since citations seem to be associated more closely with Finerty's 1926 glossary of criminal behaviour. And what of the spike in recent decades? Are we witnessing a revival of poor parenting and marital misbehaviour?

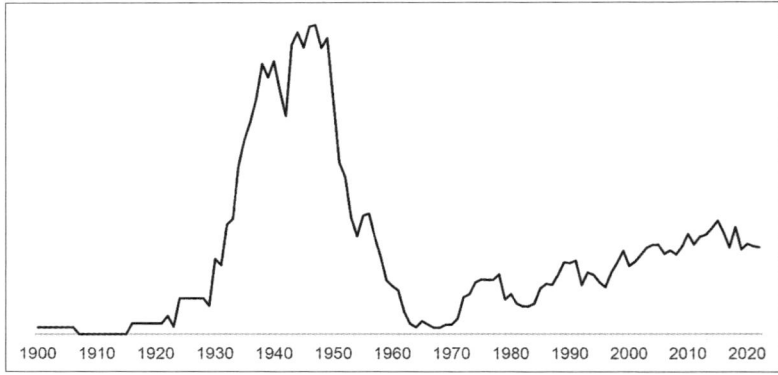

This Book is NOT

DOG-TIRED

Dog-tired reflects a state of almost complete exhaustion. It is believed to have originated during the reign of King Alfred the Great who ruled Wessex in the 9th century. Alfred was the greatest king of the Anglo-Saxons, successfully repelling waves of Viking invaders. Two of his sons (Edwin and Æthelweard) and three of his daughters (Aethelflaed, Aethelgifu and Aelfthryth) survived their childhood. Alfred would routinely send Edwin and Æthelweard out hunting with packs of dogs. The two boys would return 'dog-tired' and whichever son had been more successful would have the right to sit at their father's right hand side during dinner that evening.

As is often the case, the first use of an idiom in English can be traced back to Shakespeare. In *The Taming of the Shrew*, 1594, 'O master, master, I have watch'd so long That I am dog-weary!'.

WHEN I AM DOG-TIRED

Dogs are known for their ability to sleep for up to 16 hours a day, which is twice as much as the average human. I guess I am a pretty average human so there comes a point where my mind just rambles, I've long since lost control of it. Like a dog which has suddenly managed to slip its leash, now it's running after everything, sniffing and burrowing, chasing and rolling. What should have been a controlled process with me setting some kind of boundaries and direction has turned into me being taken for a walk. A completely random one.

Maybe that's why they call it dog-tired, the point where you're so exhausted you can't think straight? When the 'executive function' part of your brain has picked up its coat, collected its possessions and turned off the lights on the way out? What's left is an empty building full of corridors and offices scanned by one of those video surveillance systems which gives you a few seconds glimpse before moving on. A bank of screens, each flickering away with its grainy images, driven by some kind of programmed search sequence to which you don't have access.

Movement is automatic but essential. What I've learned from moments like these is that no matter how hard my arms are aching I mustn't stop. There is no option of taking the weight off my feet with a little rest in a chair, perhaps a swift doze. Because no sooner will I have sighed into my seat than the bundle I've been carrying will stir, stretch and wake. And then whatever short-term relief I might feel is replaced by panic mode as I do everything I can to forestall the inevitable. I drag myself to my feet again, desperately (but somehow also gently) jiggling and bouncing my payload in a futile attempt to lull it back to sleep. Even as I feel it drawing in air, hauling in enough fuel for the yell which is about to burst open the silence in the room.

So instead I keep going, my route circling the small space like a pris-oner pacing out his cell. The rhythm of my shuffling feet pads out a drum-beat and snatches of song dutifully rise to follow. 'I'm so tired, I haven't slept a wink'—a snatch of an old Beatles song from a lifetime ago dredges up on my internal soundtrack—'so tired, my mind is on the blink'. And of course now it's on loop, churning its way round and round, burrowing into what's left of my brain.

Seeking distraction, or inspiration, or just doing what comes next, I walk to the window. Glimpsing a field of stars outside, suddenly I'm transported to an ocean where these prickles of light are all the light we have. I feel a strange kinship with the sailors on watch, we're both charged with being responsible for the fate of something more than us, other lives depend on our keeping our eyes open and our sense sharp.

Somewhere up there is Sirius, the dog-star, I should be able to pick it out, supposed to be the brightest in the night sky. They call it that, I remember reading, because it's in the constellation Canis Major, which means big dog in Latin and is said to represent one of Orion's hunting dogs.

He's the lucky one, that big dog, rewarded for his efforts on the chase by a juicy bone and the chance to doze by the fireside at his master's feet. The rest of us, just as weary, have to make do outside, howling at the moon.

Hunting dogs, sailors on watch, parents at 3am, we've got a lot in common. The same demand that we somehow stay alert, fight the droop-ing eyelids and the fogging mind. It saps the soul, never mind the body; all you can do at the end of your shift is flop down, legs splayed as they give up the unequal struggle of supporting a body too weary for more.

There's a character in Shakespeare, one of the minor roles, the sort of player who swells a progress, starts a scene or two. His job is watching, helping his master in his complex plans to woo a fair lady, plans which involve spending long hours scanning the landscape for signs of movement. I feel for Biondello, we're kindred spirits, I know just what he means when he tells the audience 'I have watched so long that I am dog-weary'. Another recruit to our club.

But all good things come to an end; even for sailors the bell sounds and summons the new watch on deck, leaving us rubbing our eyes and heading down to our hammocks. Our lives split into slices, our time so rarely our own.

John Bessant,
Professor of Innovation Studies
Devon, UK.

The two decades after World War were a period of unparalleled economic prosperity. Perhaps that is the reason why references to 'dog-tired' fell—we could sit back and relax. But didn't the deepening of globalisation after the 1980s put an end to that!

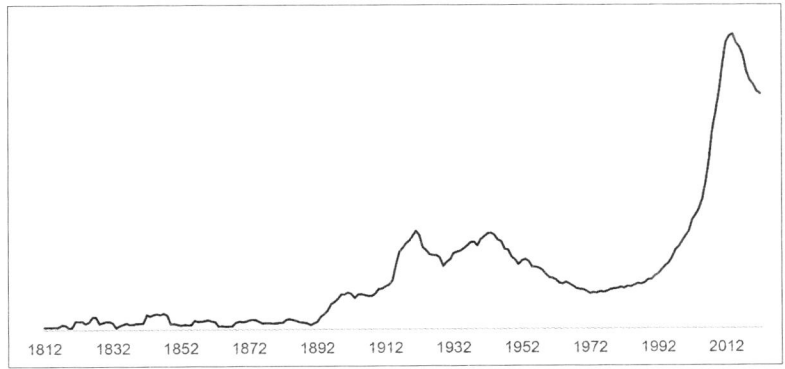

This Book is NOT

A DOG'S BREAKFAST

TO SAY something is a 'dog's-breakfast' is to say that it's a jumbled and disorganised mess. The idiom seems to have been first used in the 19th century. This was a time before dogs were fed with commercial foods, so instead of opening a can or a packet of kibble as we do nowadays, the dog would be fed a collection of scraps and left-overs. The breakfast would result in a mess, with scraps littered around the feeding bowl.

The first recorded use of this phrase was in a damming review of a play published in the London journal, *The Referee*, in November 1878: 'There is enough material for fourteen comedies crammed into its three acts, and the good things are flung together in a heap like a dog's breakfast.' More recently, the US Supreme Court chief justice John Roberts remarked on the court rulings on jury instructions that it was 'a dog's breakfast of divided, conflicting, and ever-changing analyses'.

So the phrase is now used to describe messy states such as a disorganised home, a sloppy bit of homework or writing (for example, this book!), a chaotic argument or a set of unconnected government policies. Sometimes we have some sympathy for messy ways of doing things, but if you called something a 'dog's breakfast', almost certainly you would be criticising what you saw or heard.

POOR OLD SMUDGE

We often think about the behaviour of Smudge, a bright happy Jack Russell who died almost twenty years ago. Our children found her as an abandoned puppy in the local park, and she joined our home seemingly almost without noticing the improvement from having lived rough. We tried to train her, a real necessity in London where there are significant dangers from traffic, but with limited success. She in turn tried to train us to understand what was important to her, probably too with limited success. In the end we arrived at a mutual understanding on what commands were important, sufficient for her to fit into our large and dis-organised house.

We agreed with Smudge that she should be able to roam freely on the ground floor of the house, and the garden which she accessed through a large cat flap. With some difficulty we also reached an agreement with her not to go upstairs because we would not have been able to cope with muddy pore marks on the bedding. So night-time was a lonely affair for her, sleeping in the kitchen. She compensated for her loneliness by picking up scraps of food which were invariably left on the floor (we were a family of six). For our part, we tried (with varying degrees of success) to clear up the kitchen before going to bed. Again, an accommodation that suited us all.

Friends and family often stayed overnight and our children's friends were frequent visitors. Feeding all these people was a constant challenge. Smudge of course was always ready to join in the many eating sessions and her role was to ensure that the floor was clean of food. Her meals comprised of tinned dog food and occasionally cat food when we did not manage to hold her off while the cats ate. There was a strict demarcation between human food and dog food.

On one occasion we could not face having to prepare a large meal for the horde of visitors due on the following day, so unusually we bought a roasted chicken. It was packed on a polystyrene tray and then care-fully wrapped in cling film. It looked yummy and we went to bed com-fortable that we wouldn't have to worry about cooking the next day's meal. Unfortunately, we forgot to put it in the fridge but left it on a low bench....

The next morning I came down to make tea for the late risers. Unusually, Smudge did not greet me with an enthusiastic rush and request for breakfast, a dog's breakfast. She lay in the corner, snug against the kitchen units but with a wistful look in her eye. She had an abnormally large belly and seemingly was unable to move. I tried to pick her up—she was very heavy, as heavy as a dog and a very big chicken, a polysty-rene tray and a cling film wrapping. Her belly was hugely extended. The vet feared the worst. He could not see how she could avoid fatal damage from the chicken bones, the foil, the plastic-film wrapping and the large amount of rich food. We left her with the vet where I think they applied the traditional medicine of castor oil. And then they too experienced a dog's breakfast. However, whatever it was, after a week in the dog's hospital she came home, recovered and she never looked back. But we no longer buy-in cooked chicken wrapped in a polystyrene container.

Simon Kaplinsky,
Structural Engineer (Retired)
London

Looks like dogs didn't eat many breakfasts before the mid 1950s:

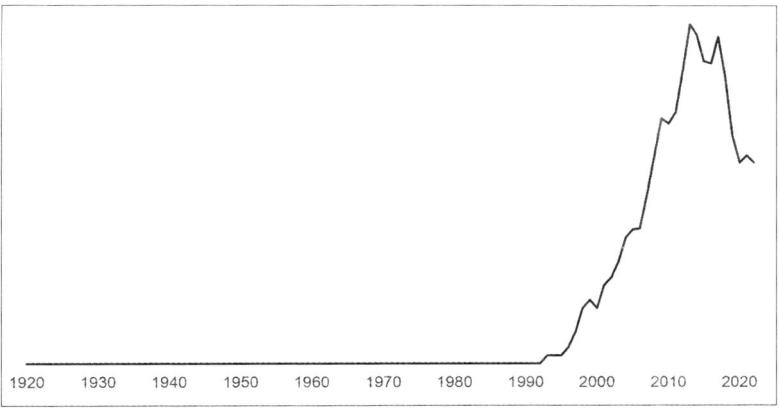

HAIR OF THE DOG

'HAIR OF a dog' is not only one of the oldest recorded idioms, but also one which is found in very many languages. No surprise, as it's most frequently used to describe cures for hangover.

Some three thousand years ago there is a reference in Ugarit, the language of Ancient Syria, to the god Ilu who cures a hangover by applying a mixture of olive oil, an unknown herb and the hair of a dog to his forehead. *A Treatise on Canine Madness* (James, 1760) marks the first recommendation that a cure for rabies could be found by placing a hair plucked from the rabid dog on the bite-wound, although James did not explain how one could extract a hair from the tail of a rabid dog without being bitten further. James in fact preferred a more effective cure for rabies which was the application of the ashes of river crabs. Although attractive options, neither of these methods have been tested for efficacy in curing rabies.

Nowadays the idiom is used generically to describe a situation in which what hurts you can cure you. In fact this is the principle underlying homoeopathic medicine—the cure for a malady is to be found in 'treating like with like'. More frequently though, the hair of a dog is used to describe the specific practice of ridding yourself of a hangover by topping up in the morning with a tipple of the same drink that has given you a pounding headache. Or, more likely, its an excuse you give to others when you are caught at the bottle the morning after.

The first recorded use of the idiom to cure a hangover can be found in Heywood's book on Proverbs written in 1546, *A Dialogue conteinyng the number in effect of all the Prouerbes in the English tongue*—'I pray thee let me and my fellow have a haire of the dog that bit us last night'.

Since alcohol, and an excessive intake of alcohol, is not specific to any one culture, it is no surprise that in one form or another, the idea than hangovers can be cured by a morning-after tipple surfaces in very many languages. This includes French, Spanish, Hungarian, Portuguese, Polish, Bosnian, Bulgarian, Croatian, Serbian, Slovenian, Russian, Turkish, German, Japanese, Dutch, Finnish, Norwegian, Afrikaans, Korean and Swahili.

HANGOVERS ARE NOT ONLY A RESULT OF TOO MUCH ALCOHOL

In my freshman year at UC Berkeley I was puzzled where I fitted on the political spectrum. My family back in LA was quite conservative; our uncle wanted all of us to join him in the John Birch Society. Just two months later, October 1962, Khrushchev delivered some advanced missiles to Cuba and I realised I had some skin in the game. Politics was probably the most likely conversation topic you would overhear on the cable cars, coffee shops and restaurants in the Bay Area, especially after Cuba.

Among the flyers handed out on campus that winter was one calling for a demonstration at the Sheraton Palace Hotel, at that time the City's premier luxury hotel (President Warren Harding died in the hotel's Presidential Suite in August 1923). There were only two demands; a significant pay raise for the 'help' who cleaned the rooms, cooked the meals, and served the guests, and real promotional opportunities for those working in the lower-paid jobs. A little research told me that about 90% of those denied a decent wage and chance for advancement were black, while management was more than 95% white.

My roommate and I went to that demonstration. The Sheraton Palace management simply ignored us. Even the cops keeping a watchful eye seemed bored. The organizers (our group was called the Ad Hoc Committee, which gives you an idea of how seriously they took the need to have an organization) decided there was no point if we could be easily ignored. Next time as we were circling the two sides of the hotel we decided to go inside and march through the lobby. Then we began singing; 'Ain't Gonna Let Nobody Turn Me Around'.

Even then the hotel management refused to meet with us. The next time through the lobby, we took a page from our brothers in the South. We sat down. That got the attention of the guests and, through them, management. They asked us to leave. They asked us to be quiet. We did neither. They called the cops, who started to arrest those sitting near the doors. But as soon as they arrested a few, more jumped in to take their place. There were maybe 600-700 of us. The cops, and then management realised they couldn't arrest all of us. During all this time the guests were getting more upset; they were paying big bucks to dine and relax in luxury. Now they had to wade through scruffy activists singing protest songs. TV and newspaper cameramen were documenting police and demonstrators scuffling at the Palace Hotel. They even published our short list of demands.

Negotiations lasted all through the night. As dawn was breaking on the second day of our sit-in, an announcement was made that our demands would be met, and the other major hotels in the city would adopt the same guidelines. My roommate and I walked outside and celebrated with the *other demonstrators. Sure, we were all sleep-deprived but we felt this had been a political breakthrough. Some of the protesters were laughing, some were crying. It was a wonderful feeling.*

Over the past 60+ years there have been many demonstrations; against the wars in Vietnam, Cambodia, Iran, Iraq, Afghanistan, and the innumerable clandestine wars in Africa and South America, as well as the murders of blacks and people of colour. I've tried to see progress where possible, but I have to admit, since 2016, it has been a lot harder to see that 'arc of justice' bending as it should. Why do I keep going to demonstrations? I want to think it's because that arc needs to bend a lot more. But if that demonstration at the Sheraton Palace hadn't been successful, would I still be at it?

I keep chasing that high.

Hugh Fowler
Santa Cruz, USA.

Wouldn't it be nice if the citations of 'hair of the dog' showed us that references to curing a hangover by drinking yet more alcohol declined during the period of prohibition in the US in the 1920s? No such luck since the decline in usage seems to have preceded the prohibition era. Perhaps, instead, the use of the idiom actually led to prohibition? Mmm, now that's a good topic for a scientific study, accompanied of course by frequent practical experimentation.

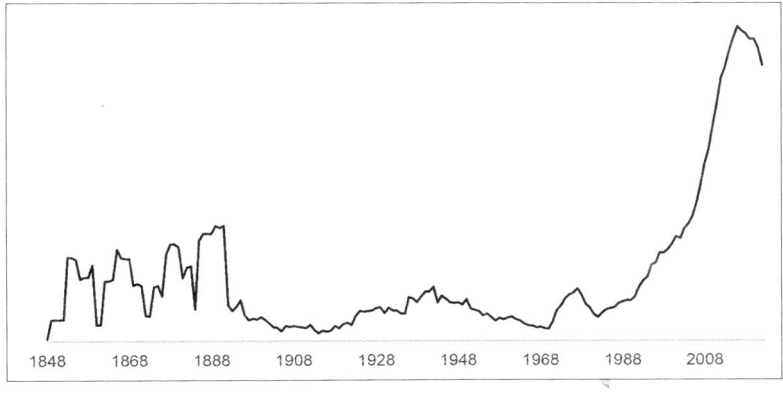

THE DOG ATE MY HOMEWORK

YOU ARE a teacher. Your most difficult pupil—the one who *never* performs in the way you would like—has failed to bring in her homework. You are tired, the week has been long, and the same student has let herself down—again. 'And please tell me why you haven't done your homework?' 'Well, Miss [your name never gets a mention with this pupil], the thing is ... [now some hesitation] ... the dog ate my homework'. Do you believe that? Of course not, it's a rubbish excuse, and in truth even the pupil doesn't expect you to believe it.

So this idiom is used to describe a ridiculous excuse for someone not doing what they were supposed to do.

The fact is that you cannot prove that this pupil's excuse is rubbish. It just so obviously seems to be the case and is an absurd way of escaping blame. So how about John Steinbeck's letter to his editor in 1922 when he apologises for the late delivery of the manuscript *Of Mice and Men* with the explanation that his red setter had eaten half of the script? Surely, surely we believe Steinbeck...

The first known mention of this idiom was in *The Cambrian* in 1905, a magazine for Welsh Americans. Its music critic referred to a Minister in a country church in Wales who was assured by his clerk that despite his fears, his sermon was indeed long enough—'I am very glad to hear you say that', he says, 'because just before I started to come here my dog got hold of my sermon and ate some of the leaves'. The first use of this idiom to explain the failure of school-children to deliver homework was in the Manchester *Guardian* in 1929—'It is a long time since I have had the excuse about the dog tearing up the arithmetic homework'.

In recent years the idiom has been used by a number of illustrious people. In 1988 President Reagan responded to the US Congress's failure to sign the budget on time—'I had hoped that we had marked the end of the "dog-ate-my-homework" era of Congressional budgetary'. During the 2012 US electoral campaign, Barack Obama excoriated his rival Mick Romney's failure to appear on a children's pre-election campaign TV show *Kids Pick the President*—'"The dog ate my homework" just doesn't cut it when you're running for president'. But perhaps most famously, the idiom has been used frequently as an excuse by Bart Simpson—in one TV episode Bart is forced to actually eat his own homework to show his teacher, Mrs Krabappel, how his dog had eaten Bart's homework. In one of Gary Larson's *Far Side* strips a teacher asks a classroom of dogs 'Did anyone here not eat his or her homework on the way to school?'

In fact dogs do sometimes eat paper, and its not very good for them. Usually they eat paper because their owner has wiped their hands or nose on it and it has a recognisable scent, or because they are anxious or just plain bored with the conversations of their owners. It can also be a sign of a condition called pica in which dogs (and some humans) have an obsessive-compulsive need to eat non-food objects such as underwear, socks, pegs and so on. It surfaces in a number of symptoms such as vomiting, diarrhoea, bad breath, tenesmus (straining to have a bowel movement) and black tarry stools. So if you suffer from any of these symptoms it's probably best to see your doctor, but don't tell them you eat these objects because the dog ate your work!

SOMETIMES DOGS DO EAT HOMEWORK

Here is a true story about a dog eating a child's homework. Late in the 1980's in the UK the scandal of school beatings was reaching a peak, both because there had been some horrific cases reported (broken skin and even broken bones were not unheard of), but also because media were getting more and more interested. An organisation called the Society of Teachers Opposed to Physical Punishment (STOPP) had been established and was doing good work. In 1988 it succeeded in having corporal punishment in schools legally banned.

I was in a Whitehall pub when this vote was passed and, as a joke, suggested that the few pounds left in the STOPP account should be diverted to stopping corporal punishment of children everywhere, in homes and also in other institutions. By the time the group of us had imbibed several celebratory glasses of wine, others had joined in and the idea gained enthusiastic acceptance. I believe that this was the origin of an organisation called End Physical Punishment of Children (EPOCH). It is extraordinary to remember that this brutality was still commonplace only 35 years ago, and shaming to realise that the legal ban on corporal punishment outside schools exists in Wales, Scotland and in Ireland but not in England. Fortunately many parents and carers in England believe that hitting children at home is illegal. Long may they believe it, but when, oh when, will it become true.

STOPP was encouraging members to find out why children were being beaten. One of the schools we were concerned with was doing a lot of hitting, often for school uniform offences, but mostly for failure to complete or deliver homework on time. One particular young teacher had declared that a boy in her class, who had twice failed to deliver his homework, would suffer for it if he did it again. He did of course, turning up on the Monday morning with no homework. He was at once sent to the headteacher with a view, the class teacher assumed, to getting caned. The headteacher, conscious of our campaign asked him not only why he had not done his homework but what it had been. The schoolboy's answers were linked. He hadn't brought his homework because the dog had eaten it, and the dog had eaten his homework because it had been four cupcakes prepared for his domestic science lesson which he had left out overnight to cool.

I am happy to tell you that the cane stayed on the side of the headteacher's desk and the class teacher kept her disappointment to herself. She was one of those who had voted against STOPP!

Penelope Leach, Child Psychologist and Best Selling Author
Lewes, UK.

The pattern of citations suggests that President Reagan seems to have been responsible for causing Mick Romney, Bart Simpson and my children and grandchildren to invent ridiculous excuses for their aberrant behaviour. Another contribution to High Culture, Ronald... but your wisdom seems to be declining in fashion.

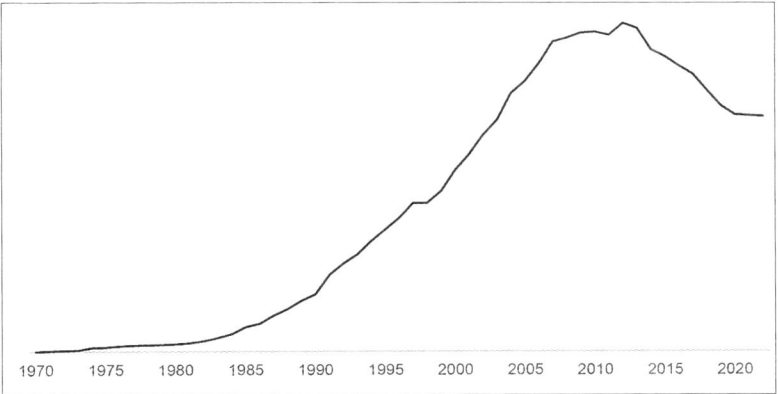

THE DOGS OF WAR

THIS IDIOM pictures the devastation caused in irregular warfare, that is, when soldiers slaughter outside of 'the rules of war'.

It is a phrase used most famously and to great effect by Mark Antony in Shakespeare's play *Julius Caesar* (1601). Shortly after Caesar's assassination by a group of senators led by Brutus, Mark Anthony, who has not taken part in the murder, is left alone with Caesar's dead body. He vows revenge for Caesar's murder and in the next scene addresses the crowd, railing against Brutus and his co-conspirators. He predicts that this will lead to riotous violence and bloodshed:

'Blood and destruction shall be so in use
And dreadful objects so familiar
That mothers shall but smile when they behold
Their infants quarter'd with the hands of war;
All pity choked with custom of fell deeds:
And Caesar's spirit, ranging for revenge,
With Ate by his side come hot from hell,
Shall in these confines with a monarch's voice
Cry 'Havoc,' and let slip the dogs of war;
That this foul deed shall smell above the earth
With carrion men, groaning for burial.

Shakespeare used a similar image in the prologue to *Henry V* in which Henry V (Harry) is compared to Mars (the Roman god of war) for his fighting prowess:

Then should the warlike Harry, like himself,
Assume the port of Mars; and at his heels,
Leash'd in like hounds, should famine, sword and fire
Crouch for employment

The hounds are likened to weapons of 'famine sword and fire' used in total warfare; releasing the 'dogs' would mean that the normal restraints of peacetime society against violence as well as the normal rules of warfare would be lifted and mayhem would ensue.

During the Middle Ages, the order to release the restraining collars of vicious dogs to set them free to hunt their prey was triggered by the order 'Havoc'. This hunting command was adopted by the English military—on the order 'Havoc', soldiers were given the licence to run amok and pillage their enemies, just as dogs were let loose to hunt without restraint. The manual of the English admiralty of 1385 (*The Black Book of the Admiralty*) included the Latin admonition *'Item, qe nul soit si hardy de crier havok'* (No one should be so foolish as to cry havoc). Shakespeare was of course familiar with this military command and used it in his depiction of Antony's chilling warning.

Another interesting allusion to the idiom Dogs of War relates to the Dominican priests central to the Spanish inquisition and who provided support to the brutal Spanish invasion of Latin America. '*Dominus*' in Latin means the 'Master/Owner/Lord' and *canis* means 'dog'. Hence the Dominican monks were characterised as 'The Hounds of God', the brutal guard dogs who hunted down heretics.

Tragically, the devastation caused by wars is central to the human experience. It is estimated that between 1900 and 2015 there were 187m victims of war globally. But when considered as a proportion of the population, that number pales into insignificance when compared with the 20-40 million deaths during the Mongol invasions and the 28-90 millions deaths in the China's Qing wars between 1850 and 1877.

But for us in modern times, 'The Dogs of War' has a much sharper meaning than the carnage resulting from 'regular warfare' (which in the Geneva Convention and other globally agreed protocols supposedly regulate the behaviour of armies and soldiers). The idiom describes a frenzy of *killing, rape and looting* rather than military set-piece conflicts, and often accompanies ethnic conflict. For example, the ethnic conflict between Hindus, Muslims and Sikhs during the separation of India and Pakistan in 1947-8 resulted in more than one million victims. In modern times the conflict between Syrian civilians and the Assad regime, Israelis and Palestinians and Ukrainians and Russians have unleashed unspeakable brutality on civilians. Mercenaries who are private individuals who fight for financial gain rather than belief, are particularly prone to behave like Shakespeare's Dogs of War.

OF, OR IN, WAR...?

So much for the Dogs of War. But what about the Dogs in War?

Between 600 BC and 20 AD the Celts and Gauls of western Europe dressed their dogs in armour and spiked collars and used them to attack the horses of their Roman invaders. Attila the Hun attacked the eastern

This Book is NOT

Roman Empire in the 5th century and used similar tactics. Mastiffs were used in the England's Wars of the Roses in the 15th century and by the armies of Prussia, England, Russia, Austria, Sweden, Saxony, Spain, Portugal and France in subsequent centuries. But as military hardware improved, and especially after guns were invented, dogs played a less prominent role in direct fighting and were instead primarily employed as trackers, messengers, sentries and companions to soldiers in battle.

In 1884 the German military established the first military dog training school and produced a military dog training manual in 1885. Soon afterwards, during the Russo-Japanese War of 1904-05, Colonel Edwin Richardson trained ambulance and guard dogs for the Russian Imperial Army. They were used to protect the Trans-Siberian railroad. Richardson later established the first army dog school in England.

These initially isolated uses of dogs in conflict subsequently led to the systematic use of dogs by all sides in the First World War. Germany prided itself in having the largest army of dogs. The corps of 28,000 dogs—mostly Alsatians—included 4,000 Red Cross ('Sanitary') dogs and 4,000 messenger and patrol dogs. Messenger dogs carried homing pigeons that were released at the front line, and telegraph dogs carried a reel with a telephone wire which unwound between battle points and command centres. The German army even used 'parachute dogs', sometimes carried by handlers and at other times falling independently. On all sides dogs were also equipped with gas-masks and the Belgian and French armies built small gun-carrying carts pulled by dogs. Precision and no barking were requirements for these tasks.

It might be thought that the growth of mechanised armour would lead to a reduction in the use of dogs in war, but it is estimated that ten times more dogs were used in WW2 than in WW1. Advanced communications technologies have reduced the contribution of dogs in warfare, and nowadays dogs are mostly used as sniffers (mines, munitions and lost soldiers) and by peacekeeping forces to separate communities in conflict.

The contributions made by individual dogs during wartime are legendary. In the early months of the bombing of London in 1940, a German Shepherd named Irma was employed as a messenger dog to carry important letters when phone lines were down. She was then trained to search *for, and rescue people after air raids during the Blitz, barking differently if bodies were dead or alive. In one famous case she stood over the body of a person who had been mistakenly declared deceased, barking that the body was 'still alive'. In another case she stood over the rubble of a bombed house for two days until two trapped girls were rescued.*

During WW2, a six-month old stray dog with a broken leg was found by soldiers in Port Darwin Australia, and was named Gunner. Gunner learned to recognise the sound of incoming Japanese planes, and so acute was his hearing that he could recognise incoming bombers 20-60 minutes before they arrived. He would bark to warn about their imminent arrival and his amazingly acute hearing was so reliable that his barking was used to sound the air-raid siren.

Raphie Kaplinsky,
Development Economist (Retired)
Barcombe Mills, UK.

This idiom seems to predominantly be literal—citations spiked during the two world wars of the 20th century. But inanimate technology now seems to have triumphed. Citations have fallen despite the wave of post-1950 wars (including Vietnam, Afghanistan, Iraq, Central Africa…). Is Shakespeare turning in his grave at this lack of literary imagination?

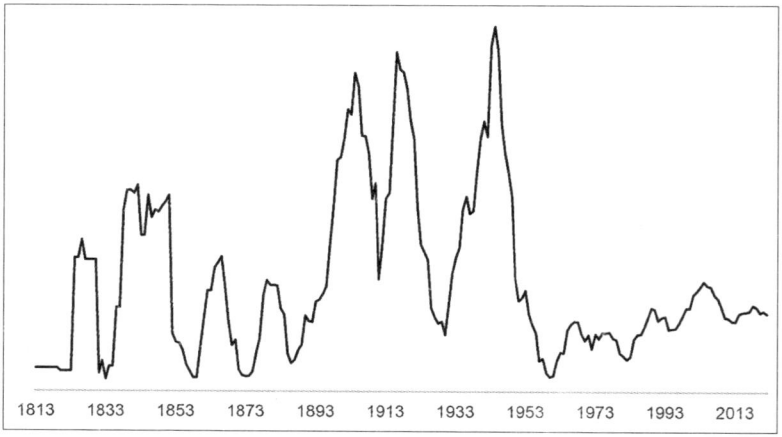

IT'S NOT THE SIZE OF THE DOG IN THE FIGHT, ITS THE SIZE OF THE FIGHT IN THE DOG

THIS IS an idiom which speaks to the importance of courage and tenacity, particularly in a conflict in which the smaller party is able to stand up against a larger or more powerful opponent. It does not only relate to physical conflict but the importance of tenacity in any struggle against seemingly more powerful odds.

Whilst its origin is unknown, what is clear is that the idiom was not, as is often claimed, created by Mark Twain, the legendary 19th century American novelist and humourist. (However Twain offered a dog-epithet which is characteristically both insightful and funny—'if you pick up a starving dog and make him prosperous, he will not bite you. This is the principal difference between a dog and a man'). The idiom originated in an article written in 1911 by Arthur G Lewis, the editor of a magazine (*Book of the Royal Blue*) given to passengers of the Baltimore and Ohio Railroad. It was rapidly picked up, and used more than 12 times before the end of the year in medical journals and trade magazines.

This idiom is widely used to encourage sports people or to describe winners of unequal sporting contests. But perhaps the best known user of this phrase was the American president Dwight Eisenhower in 1958. Reacting to pundits who predicted a hard time for his party, Eisenhower responded that 'these calculations overlook the decisive element: what counts is not the size of the dog in the fight—it's the size of the fight in the dog'.

THE POWERFUL DO NOT ALWAYS TRIUMPH

A good idiom holds multiple meanings. And the idiom in question captures much more than merely stressing the importance of courage and determination, rather than size and strength, in overcoming adversity. In talking of 'the dog', it conjures images of 'an underdog', disempowered or marginal—the cowering, whimpering, oppressed. This is an uncomfortable set of images. But it is this emphasis that appeals to me most.

The idiom encourages us to see positive change and the capacity to overcome adversity, particularly for individuals and groups who are disempowered and marginalised. This is not just wishful-thinking. Over the last 80 years or so, social psychologists have demonstrated the enormous importance and power of minority groups to lead positive change.

Researchers have shown us how important the thoughts, feelings and/or behaviours of the majority can influence our own thoughts and actions. Initially it was emphasised that we are most influenced by how the majority of group members think, feel and behave. This insight provides a valuable explanation of why, for example, seemingly ordinary people serving as guards in Nazi concentration camps acquiesced to heinous crimes against prisoners. Because people tend to follow how the majority think, feel and behave, discrimination, oppression and marginalisation often continue unchallenged and may seem difficult to resist and change.

But in fact change is possible despite the power of the dominant and framers of 'normal' values. Human history is as much a story of little people (the minority) as it is of big people (the majority). In the musical adaptation of Victor Hugo's classic historical novel—Les Misérables—set in 19th century revolutionary France, the street urchin Gavroche sings:

'And little people know
When little people fight
We may look easy pickings but we got some bite!
So never kick a dog because he's just a pup
You better run for cover when the pup grows up!
And we'll fight like twenty armies
And we won't give up'

Gavroche opens our minds to the fact that social change, and the potential for a more just and equitable world, more often comes from little people than big people.

There have been many occasions when a minority of group members—either defined by their relatively smaller numerical size or disempowered *status*—have successfully challenged the taken-for-granted view of the majority. *Social and political movements such as the Civil Rights Movement in the United States and the Freedom Movement in South Africa are good examples. Whilst minority groups are often identified with their leaders such as Martin Luther King or Nelson Mandela, they are not reducible to them. Beyond the influence of inspired leaders, social change is achieved through the individual and collective actions of minority group members, for example, through the historical civil disobedience campaigns in both the United States and South Africa.*

So, its fair to say that its 'it's not the size of the dog in the fight' that counts. Minorities do, and have, throughout history positively changed the way we think, feel and behave. But equally, 'its the size of the fight in the dog' that counts. Challenging received wisdom takes individual courage and effort. Academic research tells us that minority groups and their members are most successful in effecting change when delivering a consistent message. This needs to be presented with confidence and received as fair. When we highlight common identities amongst group members and remain flexible to compromise we are even more successful. But we must accept that these things are not easy and demand a lot of 'fight' from us.

We have all, at some stage of our lives, experienced and/or seen an injustice—for example discrimination, oppression and marginalisation—perpetrated by the seemingly more powerful. We may have felt cast as being in the minority. Yet it is when justice and equity are at stake, and recognised as such, that we need to ask ourselves not what size we are in the fight but how much fight we have. If we can find the courage and determination, or help others to do so, we can and will make a better world.

Russell Luyt, Social Psychologist
Barcombe Mills, UK.

The belligerence of dogs (and the resistance of 'small people' against the powerful) has been a *Twin Peak* phenomenon with a long period of passivity in the interim. But thankfully, the dogs and small people are back in the fight. The world is in such a mess, dominated by the malign and the odious wealthy. We need them more than ever.

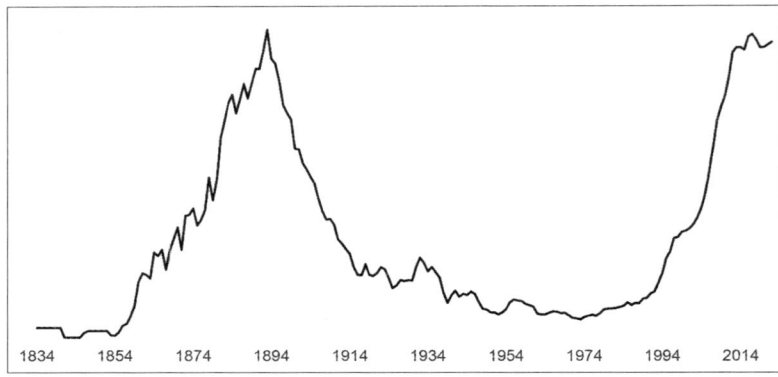

Size of the Dog in the fight

This Book is NOT

DON'T KEEP A DOG AND BARK YOURSELF

THERE ARE many reasons why you might have a dog. It could sleep on your bed and keep you warm on a cold night—in fact if its very cold you might have more than one dog on your bed; the dog might be a bribe to get your children to do their homework or to help clean the house; a dog may deter the neighbour's cats from using your garden as a toilet; or, strangely, you might actually like the company of dogs.

However, there is also a category of dog owners who need to feel protected from a hostile world—a dog might keep intruders at bay or warn you that someone unknown is approaching. And you may even want to know that the post or milk has been delivered or that your Amazon parcel has arrived. In these cases, the 'joy' of the dog is that it barks—usually loudly and too often and to the annoyance of your neighbours. But if you are keeping a dog because it barks to warn you of an impending event, why bother to bark yourself? It's a waste of effort and will only give you a sore throat.

So this idiom is used to tell someone (perhaps an employer or a nagging parent) to back off when they have delegated a task to you and then intervened to do it themselves. 'Let me be—I want to get on with my job'. And it also applies to those of us who employ a house-cleaner and then clean up before the cleaner arrives!

The tendency to meddle in delegated tasks is ubiquitous and it is not surprising therefore that its origins can be traced back some centuries. In 1583 Brian Melblancke wrote a novel called *Philotimus: the Warre Betwixt Nature and Fortune* (only three copies of the original text, which was written in the euphuistic style, have survived; euphuism is a deliberately ornate style using an excess of antitheses, alliterations and rhetorical questions). The novel includes the phrase 'It is smal reason you should kepe a dog, and barke your selfe', and it was only in the early nineteenth century that the idiom lost its euphuistic spelling. The phrase is also included in the *Compleat Collection of English Proverbs* written by John Ray in 1742.

IT IS NOT ALWAYS SENSIBLE TO LET
THE DOGS BARK FOR YOU

The art of delegation is a critical skill that requires both emotional intelligence and self-awareness and can sometimes be used to great strategic effect. The better a person is at recognising and managing these human emotions, the more effective their ability to delegate becomes. But first they may have to overcome their self-inflicted beliefs—'It's just easier to do it myself'; 'no-one can do it as well as I can, they'll mess it up'; 'there's only one way to do it'. Through good communication skills, managing expectations, patience and trust, successful leaders have learned that delegating is an essential strategic tool.

Take Clement Attlee (British Prime Minister 1945-1951) who was present at the Potsdam Conference in Germany in 1945 to negotiate the terms for the end of World War II. The atmosphere was quite different from the previous conferences at Teheran and Yalta attended by 'The Big Three'—Franklin D. Roosevelt, Winston Churchill and Joseph Stalin. President Roosevelt had died on 12 April 1945 and in his place was the new president Harry S Truman, accompanied by his newly appointed secretary of state James Byrnes. Halfway through the conference the results of the British general election were announced and Churchill and his foreign secretary Anthony Eden were replaced by the new Labour prime minister Clement Attlee and his foreign secretary Ernest Bevin. Only the leading Soviet delegates, Joseph Stalin and Vyacheslav Molotov, remained the same.

All this was totally perplexing to Stalin, who thought there must be a trick. After all, as V. M. Molotov, Stalin's foreign minister, suggested to Attlee, surely Churchill could have 'fixed' the results of the election. At Potsdam, Attlee was not at all bothered that trade-union leader Ernest Bevin, his new foreign minister, seemed to do all the talking while Attlee sat silent, wreathed in pipe smoke, nodding his head. 'You don't keep a dog and bark yourself,' he explained, 'and Ernie was a very good dog.'

In this passage from The Commanding Heights: The Battle for the World Economy *by Daniel Yergin & Joseph Stanislaw, the idiom has been used in its clear sense that when you have employed a huge army, you must not do the fighting for yourself.*

A more humorous interpretation of the idiom was offered by George W. Bush at his appearance as president of the Gridiron Club at Oxford University in March 2001. In his self-deprecating after-dinner speech he poked fun at his famous work habits, his poor speaking skills, and his reputation for delegating authority to the vice president:

And to those who say that I am dumb, lazy, inarticulate, and worst of all, a puppet who allows Dick Cheney to make all the important decisions, to those people I say… Dick, what do I say?'

It seems, though, that my mother was not as effective a delegator as either Attlee or George Bush. I grew up in Zimbabwe where my father was head of a tobacco company. My mother was kept busy by her four daughters as well as having a varied social life, which included supporting my father's (cough-cough) business life.

On this particular day she was having a tea party to introduce the wife of the new general manager who had just arrived from England to some of the other local wives. It was important to her that it all ran smoothly so she asked Susie, my sister, and me to decorate the cake while she greeted her guests.

Susie and I covered the chocolate cake with some pretty pink decorations we found tucked away in the fridge. Clearly, we thought, mum had bought them for this special occasion. We used the lot! Delighted with our creation, we presented the cake with a flourish just as mum was called away to answer the 'phone. So we did the honours and served the cake.

When mum came back, we offered her the last slice of cake. Her eyes widened, her face turned scarlet, she was speechless. She seemed about to say something, then stopped. As soon as the last guest left, she turned to us. 'Thank you, girls. I am very grateful for all your help today, There is just one small detail you need to know. The little pink decorations you used happened to be my contraceptive pills.'

So, if you are asking someone to bark on your behalf, think Attlee and Bush, not Civardi!

Anne Civardi, author and sculptor
Barcombe, UK.

This Book is NOT

'And bark yourself', which is presumably a reference to the idiom 'don't keep a dog and bark yourself' has seen a sharp revival in popularity after the 1980s. Perhaps managerial meddling has become more persistent, or perhaps more of us are employing cleaners and cleaning the house before they arrive?

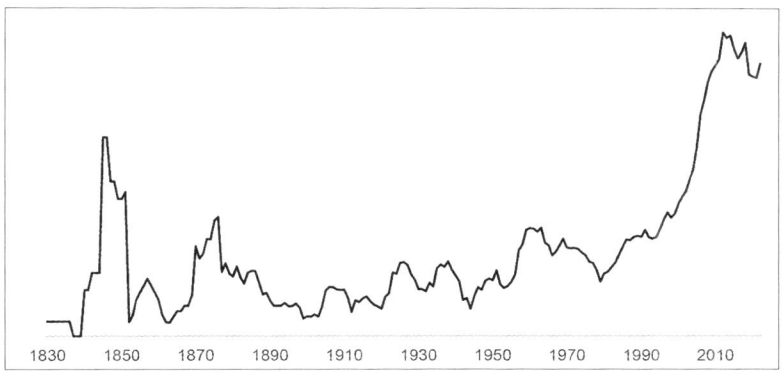

DOG DAYS

WHEN THE weather is hot—very very hot—it's the time of the dog days.

If you live in the Northern Hemisphere and you look up on a clear summer night you will be blinded by the brightest star, Sirius. Sirius is in the Canis Major ('big dog' in Latin) constellation. It is twice the size and 25 times more luminous than the sun. And if you want to visit Sirius, it is a mere 8.6 light years (51 trillion miles) from the earth. During the dog days of summer—supposedly the hottest days of the year—Sirius rises and sets at the same time as the sun.

The idea that the rising of the dog-star Sirius heralds (and indeed causes) the onset of the hottest period in summer is deeply rooted in Western culture. In Greek mythology Sirius is the dog of the hunter Orion, who has a constellation of his own next to Canis Major. In Homer's *Iliad*, written in the 8th century BC, Achilles is returning to Troy and complains about the intense heat:

> Priam saw him first, with his old man's eyes,
> A single point of light on Troy's dusty plain.
> Sirius rises late in the dark, liquid sky
> On summer nights, star of stars,
> Orion's Dog they call it, brightest
> Of all, but an evil portent, bringing heat
> And fevers to suffering humanity.
> Achilles' bronze gleamed like this as he ran

A hundred years after the *Iliad* was written, the Greek poet Alcaeus advised that before the arrival of Sirius, it was best to 'steep your lungs in wine since women are at their foulest but men are weak since they are parched in head and knees'. Even Aristotle got in the act. In his treatises *Physics*, he used the heat of the dog days of summer to explain the principles of movement. Pliny, the Roman Philosopher who lived two thousand years ago, recommended that

This Book is NOT

the way to reduce dog attacks (which he believed increased during the hot Dog Days of mid-summer) was to feed them chicken manure.

The first recorded use in German of Dog Days to describe the intense heat of mid-summer was in the 16th century. It was also in the 1500s that Dog Days entered the English language. The phrase was derived from the Latin *caniculares dies* (puppy days), which in turn was drawn from Hellenistic Greek. In 1564, *Hope of Health* suggested that purging (inducing vomiting and blood-letting) should not be practiced during the 'Dogge daies of summer because the Sunne is in Leo, and then is nature burnt up & made weake'. In 1729, Husbandman's *Practice* advised men to abstain all this time from women and to take heed of feeding violently during the dog days of summer.

Clavis Calendria, A Compendious Analysis of the Calendar, Illustrated with Ecclesiastical, Historical, and Classical Anecdotes, published in 1813, tells us about a time when the 'Sea boiled, the Wine turned sour, Dogs grew mad, Quinto raged with anger, and all other creatures became languid; causing to man, among other diseases, burning fevers, hysterics, and phrensies'.

In modern times American folklore tells us that Dog Days herald different dangers, some which are far more dangerous than 'causing frensies and feeling weak', and which cannot be held at bay by 'abstaining all this time from women'. Did you know for instance, that during the Dog Days of summer, snakes are said to go blind and be more likely to bite you, that the morning dew is poisonous to open wounds, that bacterial infections are more common and dangerous and that men and dogs are more likely to be mad? In the American south, ghosts are at work during the Dog Days, so women are advised to wash walls with vinegar, to paint the porch-ceiling blue (so that it looks like water), and men are advised to wear socks inside out and to don baseball cap backwards to avoid bad fortune. Oh, and just to be safe, make sure that you are wearing a cross around your neck. Eleanor Long's book *How the Dog Got Its Days* reminds us of the folklore which advises that during the

Dog Days 'all liquids are poisonous, when bathing, swimming, or even drinking water can be dangerous, and a time when no sore or wound will heal properly'. Even modern farmers are aware of the consequences of the Dog Days, as they are guided by decades of accumulated knowledge, witnessed in the widespread reciting of the ditty 'Dog Days bright and clear/Indicate a happy year/But when accompanied by rain/for better times our hopes are vain'.

If you live in the northern hemisphere and want to avoid these dangers during your summer vacation, then its probably best to wait a few thousand years. In the time of the Hellenic Empires before Christ, Sirius's provoking of the Dog Days coincided with the summer solstice. But due to a combination of the earth's elliptical orbit and gravitational field (this is called precession), the Dog Days are moving on. They are already now most likely to occur between the 3rd July and the 11th August and if we wait long enough, Sirius won't even be around during summer. In ten thousand years Sirius will rise in the middle of winter. But if not Sirius, who then will be responsible for provoking the onset of the Dog Days?

SCORCHING CYNOPHOBIA

Cynophobes! That's most humans every day. They hear slurs against their most faithful friend on this planet and do absolutely nothing about it— not even bat an eyelid.

I'm serious about cynophobia: dog hating by casual insult even when you think you like us and say some of my best friends are dogs. Oh no, I won't let that happen. We've watched from your knee height how human feminists and people of slighted races are now asserting themselves. Well, I'm no sleeping dog—I'm woke and I'm not lying! Us dogs are going digital—watch out for our byte!

You want evidence of how humans undermine us with slurs? You must be joking! Yes, the truth is revealed in jokes—look at this book. Such numerous insults you don't even notice them: dog's life, gone to the dogs, dog's dinner, dog eat dog, hair of the dog, dog's body, sick as a dog, dog

Cynophobia onset

returns to its vomit, lie like a dog, crooked as a dog's leg—I could go on, insult after insult! And the worst is the cynophobic cancel culture, just look at this from the New York Times: *'New York Times has cancelled 'bitch' and no longer recognises it as a valid word in its word puzzles.' So human sensitivities rule okay? At the price of us dogs: you misused the legitimate word for a female of our species to insult other humans, and now to make humans feel better you ban the word altogether! And you think we're of limited intelligence!*

But none of this is new. Ever since some slouched homo erectus gnawed a bone and tossed it towards a wolf pup who kindly wagged, somehow seeing a goodness worth following in humans—yes, it's in there some-where—humans have taken advantage of canine faithfulness and pro-jected their own failings onto dogs!

Nonsense you say? All those memorials humans have put up to honour dogs—Greyfriars Bobby of Edinburgh, Hachiko of Tokyo, Foxie of Helvellyn, Just Nuisance of Simonstown?

Well, to prove my point look at what's happened to the greatest dog memorial of all. Ancient Greeks named the brightest star in the heavens (Alpha Canis Majoris) the Dog Star to honour Orion the Hunter's dog. In the Iliad, *Homer blamed Sirius' rising before the sun for causing the sweltering heat of the Dog Days leading to lethargy, storms, fires, illness, wanton women, men weak in head and knees and vicious dogs—so feed chicken manure to calm them advised Pliny the Elder more than two thousand years ago.*

Scientific nonsense of course—heat from the Dog Star 8.6 light years distant doesn't reach Earth—but don't let that stop humans building the slur of Dog Days into their culture. 'Dog daies' of 16th century English lit-urgies have now become simply bad days;Winston Churchill's reference to his 'black dog days' is not only a slur on dogs but cultural appropriation; they even slur us in films (Dog Day Afternoon) *and music* (Dog Days are Over). *So just as human science is advancing, human culture embeds the old ignorance.*

And in a strange twist which we dogs can only watch in horror, human perversity is now making Dog Days devastation greater than ever as global warming brings worse summer temperatures and forest fires. Is the

This Book is NOT

Anthropocene writing its own epitaph—'Human Days RIP' perhaps? So if you are up early in mid-summer (3 July—11 August in 2024) and see the brightest star hanging in the pre-dawn light, remember to honour your dog and renew your commitment to stopping global warming.

Mike Hubbard, Lecturer and Researcher (Retired)
Birmingham, UK.

There is little sign that global warming is reflected in an increase in literary references to Dog Days. Do people not notice that the weather is warming up? Or perhaps we hide our shame, and stay guiltily silent just in case we jinx the heat.

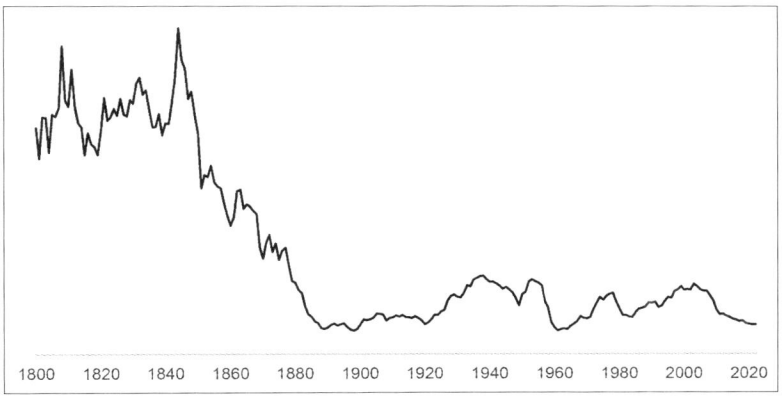

DOG WHISTLE POLITICS

DOGS HAVE both better and different hearing to humans. They can pick up sounds much better than we can, from further away (four times the distance) and they can more easily differentiate between sounds. Critically, they can also hear much higher-pitched sounds. This is because they have 18 different muscles in their ears compared to the six possessed by humans and have longer ear canals to channel sound. With 30 ear muscles, cats have even better hearing than dogs. So whilst dogs can hear high pitches up to 45 kilohertz per second (40kHz), and cats up to 64 kHZ, a human baby's hearing only stretches to 20 kHz, and then declines to 15-17 kHz in old age.

In the house or the garden we can get the attention of dogs by calling their names or by making sounds such as whistling. But in the open, when the distance between animal and human is large, some other form of provoking attention is required. In pre-Civil War America dogs were used to hunt down escaped slaves and were controlled by whistles. These loud whistles not only recalled the dogs but terrified the hunted slaves. The development of ultrasonic whistles—emitting sounds at such a high pitch that they cannot be picked up by the human ear—is attributed to Charles Darwin's colleague Francis Dalton in 1876. Dalton was engaged in experiments to measure the hearing capacity of different animals as part of his general concern to prove that ability is inherited. He began with animals and then turned his attention to humans, asserting that people of colour were intellectually inferior to white people as a consequence of their genetic inheritance.

How ironic, therefore, that Dalton's ultrasonic whistle has in recent years become a metaphor for the politics of racism. The idiom dog whistle politics was first recorded in 1947 in Robert Puth's *American Economic History* referring to a speech by Franklin Delano Roosevelt as being designed to be like a modern dog whistle, with a note so high that the sensitive farm ear would catch it perfectly while the unsympathetic East would hear nothing. It

This Book is NOT

entered contemporary mainstream political discussion in the late 1980s to describe the use of coded images designed to reach a selected audience without the appearance of overt prejudice. These targeted coded messages are invariably used by right-wing, racist, anti-Semitic and anti-Islamic political demagogues.

THE DOG WHISTLE DOMINATES OUR CURRENT POLITICS

There is a long history of dog whistle tropes targeted to attack particular ethnicities. Perhaps the most infamous are those which are anti-Semitic such as The Protocols of the Elders of Zion *published in the late 19th century. It purported to report more than 20 meetings held in Basle, Switzerland in 1897 in which Jews and Freemasons conspired to undermine Christian civilization by spreading liberalism and socialism through Europe. The document asserted that a cabal of international Jewish financiers and bankers ruled the world of economics and politics. The word cabal is drawn from the kabbalah, a mystical interpretation of the Hebrew Bible; and global or international financiers spoke to a world of the greedy rich who had no loyalty to any nationality.* The Protocols of Zion *was central to the narrative of anti-Semitism in Europe before the First World War and was actively used in Nazi Germany; Henry Ford, the inventor of mass production distributed copies to his workforce and 92 editions of his* Dearborn Independent *newspaper sought to expose the Jews' 'financial and commercial control, usurpation of political power, monopoly of necessities, and autocratic direction of the very news that the American people read'. Its central message was that the 'International Jew and his satellites' was the cause of the world's problems, such as labour unrest, Bolshevism, financial panics and wars. So whilst the anti-Semitic dog whistle calls out against international financiers and bankers and globalists, they mean Jews who were attacking capitalism and the wealthy. The message is currently heard, relayed and amplified by anti-Semites on X, tik-tok and other social media.*

In the modern era, dog whistle politics are closely associated with the rise of Donald Trump. Detailed textual analysis of his speeches identify six key terms which he uses in a vague manner but which have the function of alerting his targeted audience to an active hatred of political opponents who challenge inequality, racism, xenophobia, and the abuse of power. So, 'law and order' evokes images of black Americans roaming the streets and committing acts of murder and theft; 'school choice' speaks to the same racism and calls for resistance to the redistribution of income and power; 'illegal migrants' addresses the fear of white America being overwhelmed by Latin American and Muslim migrants; 'welfare' targets the poor and black communities who are seen to make disproportionate claims on government budgets which are 'paid' by white Americans; 'Islam' conflates religious affiliation with terrorism and deliberate attempts by the Muslim population to have more children in order to overwhelm white Americans by number; and 'voter identification' is a call for voter suppression to reduce electoral support for Democrat candidates. In itself none of these six dog whistles is offensive and each has a general meaning which carries no wider content. But to Trump and his supporters, each of these dog whistles evokes an image of non-white, non-Christian and godless enemies. Like dogs and cats this audience hears and acts on things which others do not.

But Trump was not the pioneer of modern American dog whistle politics. The famous Republican Party strategist supporting Ronald Reagan's bid for the presidency observed that although the word 'nigger' might have been acceptable in 1954, this was regrettably not the case in 1968. So, instead, he used the phrase 'states' rights' as a code for the legitimisation of the racist policies prevalent in the American South. Atwater advised that since it was not legitimate to use the word 'nigger', 'You say stuff like, uh, forced busing, states' rights'.

In the UK the Brexit campaign used a poster showing waves of people in a queue, suggesting that they were a horde of mostly illegal immigrants seeking to enter Britain and this was a consequence of membership of the EU. It is striking that the only white face in this queue was blocked out by the text box Leave the EU. In other words, the dog whistle queue was being used to appeal to an audience which included a large number of people who were also racists and anti-Islamist.

The child abuse case in Rochdale UK in which nine men were

This Book is NOT

convicted in 2012 was widely used by Conservative politicians to exploit and stir racial antagonism for electoral advantage. Then home secretary Suella Braverman claimed that 'almost all members' of these gangs were British Pakistani men who held attitudes 'incompatible with British values'; the prime minister, Rishi Sunak, said victims had been ignored by police and social workers and that this 'was due to cultural sensitivity and political correctness' and he went on, 'that is not right'. These dog whistle claims were made despite the fact that a Home Office Report concluded that no community was disproportionately represented in the grooming gangs. And even if it were true that a disproportionate number of the Rochdale abusers were Muslim men, does the extensive child moles-tation which existed in the Catholic church throughout Europe, North America and Australia prove that white men are the primary culprits of child abuse? Of course not. But it depends on which audience you are talking to and who has the intent and capacity to listen to the particular trope which you are promoting.

Raphie Kaplinsky, Development Economist (Retired)
Barcombe Mills, UK

Donald Trump? Brexit? Victor Orban? Why else has there been such as spurt in the use of this idiom in recent years?

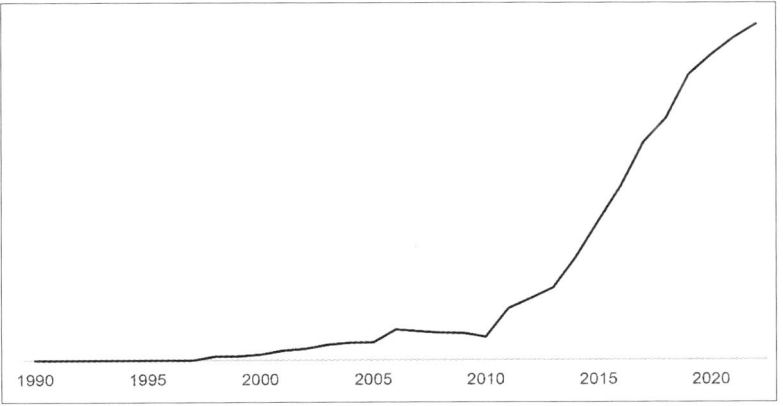

DOG NIGHT

THERE IS cold, and there is very cold. And then there is very, very cold which is how it is at night in Alaska, with temperatures sometimes falling below -45°C. The Eskimo peoples live in these freezing conditions, so how do they manage to keep warm at night? For one thing it appears that some Siberians and Native Americans benefit from a gene variant which is a similar to a gene sequence found in the Denisovans, an extinct human species who once ranged between Siberia and Southeast Asia. This unique gene seems to offer some protection from extreme cold. However, Eskimos also make protective clothing from the skins of caribou, seals, deer and moose. Although polar bear skins provide very warm clothing, they are too thick to move around in, so the skins are mostly used for blankets. Living in igloos also helps keep the extreme cold at bay. Whilst the ice walls don't give off any heat, they keep the wind out and share the body heat (and no doubt body odours) between fellow igloo inhabitants.

By contrast it gets very, very hot in the Australian outback, with the temperature sometimes exceeding 45°C. But it is not always exceedingly hot in the outback. On occasions it gets rather cold at night in winter. With the wisdom of modern technology, the Isla Hotel in the Australian outback recommends that its winter visitors dress warmly and, if they are sleeping outside, use sleeping bag liners. So how did the indigenous Aboriginal peoples, ignorant of the Isla Hotel's technological sophistication, keep warm in winter? They coped by making coats from possum skins, and covered their bodies with grease from porcupines, possums, mutton-birds and penguins.

The power of human ingenuity transcends the vast distances between northern and southern hemispheres and provides a much more comforting technique to keep warm. The Eskimo peoples in North America, Greenland and Siberia and the Aboriginal peoples in Australia realised that having a dog sleeping on your bed—in fact more than one dog—not only soothed their troubles and kept bad

This Book is NOT

dreams at bay, but also kept them warm. Thus the measure they used to calibrate the cold was not degrees Fahrenheit or Celsius, but the number of dogs needed to sleep on their bed to keep them warm. It could be three and even four or five dogs, but the ubiquity of the 'three dog' idiom follows from the popularity of a famous band in the 1970s, called 'The Three Dog Night'.

THE WISDOM OF CHILDREN

Of the twelve or so dogs that have come and gone in my life, none was ever allowed to sleep on the bed.

It may seem an odd family rule, especially after I explain that our mother savagely sorted others' households by those with couches that could absorb wet dogs (old money, thus good families) and those who could not (new money, therefore bad families). But it's family, and every family has its idiosyncrasies. In my family, these mostly trace back to the things my mother believed and said, how she limned the world based upon those beliefs and what happened next.

Familial beliefs are the real stuff of inheritances, of course, and weigh more heavily upon us than any heirloom tea service or cherished cocktail ring. Those things we merely lust after, manoeuvre to get, or beg for, and while they may splendidly decorate our table—or us—they are mere embellishment. Familial idiosyncrasies, on the other hand, penetrate, replicate and continue to pass along like DNA.

Perhaps few things shake us as substantially as saying no to these inheritances—refusing to take delivery, as it were, to what we would otherwise absorb. We're given opportunities every day to do so, of course—to simply stop believing something a parent believed—but we mostly miss those chances in the comfortable haze of repetition, obligation and loyalty. So we continue on, buffered by the things we heard, said and did at home.

Then, if we marry, we are gifted with a chance to question, shed or combine some of our essential ideas. But I went a fairly long time without being married, having been frequently told along the dating path that I believed some fairly screwy stuff about relationships and compatibility.

My parents took separate vacations, for instance, and so I asserted that, too, to be the right way of things—like not welcoming a dog into your bed.

When I got to be about 33, I met a man who had never had a dog, so I married him and set about to change that, as well as some other beliefs and habits of his that I quickly perceived as odd. Immediately, however, he had his own set of rules about our first canine companion. This included no dogs on the bed. There, at least, we were compatible. So despite living in the cold climate of what some Americans cheerfully call the Great Northeast, dog after dog remained in their own beds, and we in ours, as we worked our way through a marriage.

When I became a mother at 40 and began the careful process of putting into place what had been put into place for me, my husband asked me if I thought that some of the things I believed might need to go. I didn't. None of them. Not then.

But children assess the world they're plopped into with the unique ability to spot the ridiculous, the ingrained and the absurd.

'Who makes these rules?' our daughter asked one Sunday after I had slipped her tiny feet into tight patent leather Easter shoes with a warning that she absolutely could not wear them after June 1. Well, I thought, I didn't know who made these rules. But I knew who taught them to me and just how many of them rolled off my tongue—and bounced off my child like Silly Putty. She was that kind of a child, thankfully. 'Why?' she would ask, and as she did, each one got held up to the light and, one after another, got tossed like a girdle I now not only cannot believe I ever wore, but breathe better without.

Then one Christmas we surprised our daughter with an invitation to a sled dog camp for New Year's Eve. We would go to the very top of New England, where it is almost always cold, to an area known as The Northeast Kingdom—a thickly forested land known mostly to wilderness fishing enthusiasts, hunters and a sturdy few residents. The camp was 10 miles off the road, all of which we drove in a blizzard, arriving around dinner time. As we pulled in, the headlights revealed dogs. Everywhere. For we had arrived at the only 'unchained' dog-sled camp in the country, where the dogs are free to roam on the 140 acres. For three glorious days, you can live among them—eating with them, sledding with them daily and helping to care for them.

And every night, you are allowed to choose the dogs you'd like to have accompany you to your cabin. That first night was nearly 35 degrees below zero, and as the four dozen or so dogs swirled around us, our daughter pointed to a sleek brown and black hound mix named Waffles. None of the dogs here are traditional sled dogs. Many have been rescued. Waffles joyously trotted with us into our cabin. He jumped onto our daughter's bed and then looked over at her. She giggled. She turned to me.

'Can he sleep in my bed?'

Why did this feel like the last of the rules to go? Maybe it was.

'Absolutely'

Marion Roach Smith, Memoir Coach and Author
New York State, USA.

It seems that that it was only after 1960 that modern 'civilised' society rediscovered the technology of using dogs to keep warm at night, although enthusiasm seems to have waned recently. Or perhaps references to this idiom reflect the fact that songs by Three Dog Night are not included in the Spotify collection.

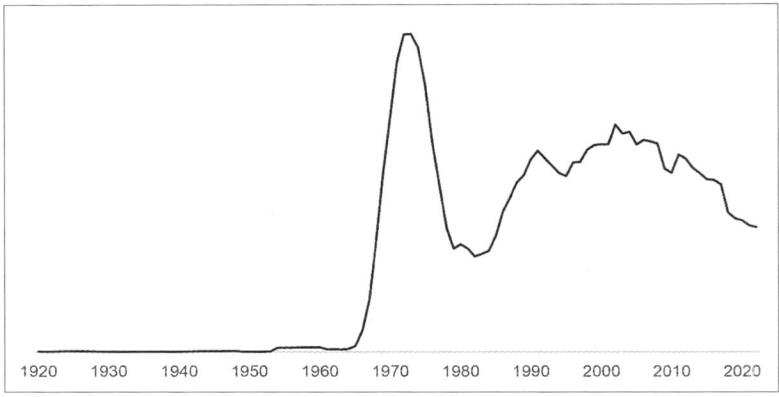

DOG-EARED

THE PHRASE 'dog-eared' refers to the practice of folding over a corner of a page to allow the reader to revisit that passage. When this has been done a number of times, the folded section becomes soiled and limp and curls over 'like a dog's-ear'. Can dog-eared pages be repaired? No, because the crease harms the fibres of the paper. But the severity of the 'dog-eared' damage depends on the number of times the ear is used, the quality and age of the paper and whether the page is contaminated with dust and dryness. It is possible to make a noticeable difference to the dog-ears by using an iron and some blotting paper to dissipate the heat and this is the method used by many librarians of old and valued books

However, 'dog-eared' does not only describe what a much-used book page looks like. It is also an idiom with a wider meaning, describing any repetitive action which leaves a noticeable trace. It is also used to describe things which are 'worn' and 'unkempt'.

One of the earliest recorded uses of the phrase was by a German poet, Andreas Gryphius, in the early 17th century. Andreas had a troubled life, living through the Thirty Years War in Silesia. He was traumatised by the carnage of the war, and amongst his more famous poems are those entitled 'All is Vanity and Human Misery' (neither of which by the way, have much relevance to the phrase 'dog-eared', but aren't they intriguing titles?) It is probable that dog-eared books were more common in Gryphius's time since the printing press was only invented in Europe in the 15th century so individual books were read and reread on numerous occasions.

'Dog-eared' was first recorded in English is by William Hawkings in 1627. Hawkins, a schoolmaster and poet with frustrated ambitions to teach at Cambridge, wrote a play for his pupils at Hadleigh Grammar School in Suffolk. Despite the inclusion of the 'dog-ears' idiom in the script, the play never registered as a best-seller. We do not know if the contemporaneous use of dog-ears in these two countries was connected, and nor if their origins go back further to a common root.

Irma Pince, librarian at Hogwarts School of Witchcraft and

Wizardry, is a prominent hater of those who dog-ear books in her care—'A warning if you rip, tear, shred, bend, fold, deface, disfigure, smear, smudge, throw, drop, or in any other manner damage, mistreat, or show lack of respect towards this book, the consequences will be as awful as it is within my power to make them'.

Nowadays, not only are books freely available, but for many readers they have been superseded by electronic media. So what is the equivalent of a dog-ear for a book read on the internet, a computer or a telephone? Perhaps 'bookmark' is the modern-day computer equivalent, and 'favourites' in the case of photos in a photo-album? However unlike the paper medium, 'bookmarks' and 'favourites' do not get worn over time, do not show overuse and are not in need of repair, with or without an iron. There is no dog ear on our screens!

DOG-EARED PREJUDICES

I have a haunting personal experience of the phrase 'dog-eared' which has no relevance to its use as an idiom in the English language. But so what—it is one of my more vivid memories of my childhood! I was brought up in South Africa during the terrible years of apartheid, when there were punishing, unjust and legal barriers discriminating between people of different colour. Those with whiter skins led privileged lives, supported by the exploited labour and the suffering of those with darker skins. Amongst the white population were the largely rural tribe of Afrikaners, descendants of the Dutch settlers who colonised the southern tip of Africa in the 16th century. After they won the election in 1948 (only white people could vote), the poorly educated Afrikaner population legalised and intensified the racial barriers and exploitation that had been a feature of South Africa since the first settlement by Europeans in 1652. They also introduced a series of measures designed to perpetuate their hold on power. This included forcing schools to teach Afrikaans. In 1976 this edict was the instigation for mass protest by black schoolchildren against apartheid. It led to many of them being shot, tortured and imprisoned. But it was one

This Book is NOT

of the most important factors leading to the overthrow of the apartheid system of racial oppression.

I was brought up to scorn Afrikaners, despising their ideology and disparaging their 'ignorance' and poor levels of education. Nevertheless it was impossible to escape their drive to bring all whites into their laager (a phrase referring to the defensive encirclement of ox-wagons to defy the resisting indigenous population). And this meant that I, like every child, was forced to learn Afrikaans at school. I only remember two of the literary materials which they forced down our throats. One was a text prescribed during my years at secondary school called Drie Swerwers oor Die Einders, a worthy but impenetrable book with small print-type which I think described the plight of survivors of a shipwreck on the West Coast of what is now Namibia. I knew that Swerwers meant 'wanderers', but to this day have no idea of what 'einders' means or indeed what the book was about. But more relevant to the idiom 'dog-ears' was a poem which I learnt and loved during my years of early primary schooling. Why did I love it? Of course, because it was about a dog. And what relevance does it have to the phrase 'dog-eared'? Read the poem by Jan Fe Celliers and the translation below and see. And in so doing, share my nostalgia about a childhood in which my own prejudice blinded me to the fact that all people, even the wicked Afrikaners who implemented the iniquitous system of apartheid, have similar human feelings. Shame on me!

Wag-Hondjies	*Watch Dogs*
„Oppas!' het die baas gesê,	'Be alert!' the master said
„tot ek weer kom, hier bly lê!'	'Until I return, lie here!'
Op ons pootjies lê ons kop,	On our paws, we put our head,
maar ons hou jou darem dop,	but we still keep an eye on you
toe-oog slaap ons op die baadjie,	eyes closed we sleep on the jacket
maar ons loer nog deur 'n gaatjie—	but we still squint through a little gap
één oor plat, en één oor op,	one ear down, one ear up,
pas-op!	Be alert!'

Raphie Kaplinsky, Development Economist, (Retired)
Barcombe Mills, UK.

It looks like the phrase 'dog-ears' came into fashion after the 1980s but its popularity declined after the financial crisis of 2008. Why the recent decline? Perhaps the financial crash meant that fewer people were writing—or reading—books because they were panicking on their computer screens, wondering whether they should jump out of their windows as their predecessors were rumoured to have done in the Great Crash of 1929. Or perhaps we should be looking at their bookmarked tabs:

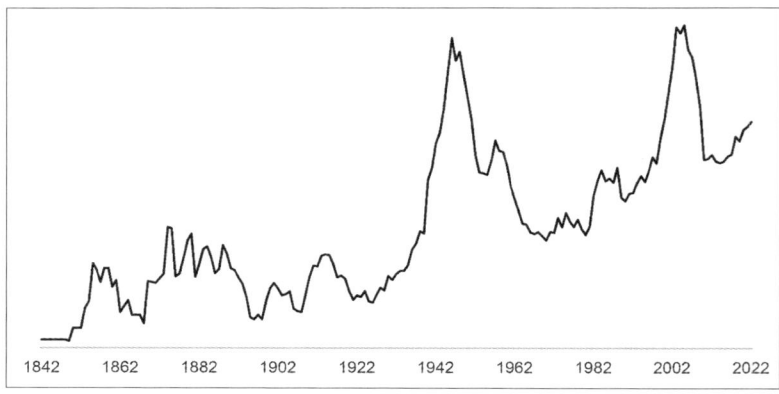

This Book is NOT

MAD DOGS AND ENGLISHMEN

IT IS sometimes asserted that the phrase Mad Dogs and English-men can be traced back to Rudyard Kipling, but this is mistaken. The phrase is found in a travelogue written by Charles Burney in 1870 and repeated in amongst other texts in Melville's *The Adventures of a Griffin on a Voyage of Discovery* written in 1867.

The Idiom *Mad Dogs and Englishmen go out in the Midday Sun* is closely associated with Noël Coward, the English playwright, lyricist and performer. Coward was born in 1899 in Middlesex and died as a tax exile in Jamaica in 1973. He was the son of an impe-cunious piano tuner and had little formal education but achieved considerable wealth and fame, leading an extravagant public life. At the onset of the Second World War he ran Britain's propaganda office in Paris but with little success—'if the policy of His Majesty's Government is to bore the Germans to death I don't think we have time'.

Coward wrote the song 'Mad Dogs and Englishmen' during a car journey in Vietnam, committing it to memory since he was without pen and paper

> 'I wrestled in my mind with the complicated rhythms and rhymes of the song until finally it was complete, without even the aid of pencil and paper. I sang it triumphantly and unaccompanied to my travelling companion on the verandah of a small jungle guest house. Not only [my travelling companion], but the gecko lizards and the tree frogs gave every vocal indication of enthusiasm'.

First performed in 1931 in New York, the song is a parody of the foolishness and eccentricity of British colonials and fittingly, opens with the first ten notes of Rule Britannia. It has to be delivered as a fast-spoken verse, with deliberate spelling errors ('persprie' and 'ultry-violet') to maintain the rhyming flow. Coward's mockery of Englishness no doubt was drawn from his observations of the world of effete, patrician haughtiness and snobbery in which he socialised.

In tropical climes there are certain
    times of day
When all the citizens retire to tear
    their clothes off and persprie.
It's one of those rules that the
    greatest fools obey,
Because the sun is much too sultry
And one must avoid its ultry-violet ray.
The native grieve when the white
    men leave their huts,
Because they're obviously

definitely nuts!

Mad dogs and Englishmen
Go out in the midday sun,
The Japanese don't care to.
The Chinese wouldn't dare to,
Hindoos and Argentines sleep
    firmly from twelve to one.
But Englishmen detest a siesta.
In the Philippines there are lovely
    screens

To protect you from the glare.
In the Malay States there are hats
    like plates
Which the Britishers won't wear.
At twelve noon the natives swoon
And no further work is done.
But mad dogs and Englishmen
Go out in the midday sun.

It's such a surprise for the Eastern
    eyes to see
That though the English are effete,
They're quite impervious to heat,
When the white man rides every
    native hides in glee,
Because the simple creatures hope he
Will impale his solar topee on a
    tree.
It seems such a shame when the
    English claim the earth
That they give rise to such hilarity
    and mirth.

Mad dogs and Englishmen
Go out in the midday sun.
The toughest Burmese bandit
Can never understand it.
In Rangoon the heat of noon
Is just what the natives shun.
They put their Scotch or Rye
    down, and lie down.
In a jungle town where the sun
    beats down

To the rage of man and beast
The English garb of the English
    sahib
Merely gets a bit more creased.
In Bangkok at twelve o'clock
They foam at the mouth and run,
But mad dogs and Englishmen
Go out in the midday sun.

Mad dogs and Englishmen
Go out in the midday sun.
The smallest Malay rabbit
Deplores this foolish habit.
In Hong Kong they strike a gong
And fire off a noonday gun
To reprimand each inmate
Who's in late.
In the mangrove swamps
Where the python romps
There is peace from twelve till two.
Even caribous lie around and
    snooze;
For there's nothing else to do.
In Bengal to move at all
Is seldom, if ever done.
But mad dogs and Englishmen
Go out in the midday
Out in the midday, out in the
    midday,
Out in the midday, out in the
    midday,
Out in the midday, out in the
    midday sun!

YES, THE ENGLISH REALLY ARE ECCENTRIC

This idiom draws our attention to two aspects of British history and culture. The first reflects the arrogance and cultural insensitivity of the British, as widely evidenced during the long centuries of colonial rule. One example of this was the stupidity of the British colonial army during the South African Boer War of 1899-1902. Dressed in bright red uniforms and shiny white pith helmets, the British troops were easy targets for the Boer guerrilla fighters. Their red uniforms had inadequate collars to protect the troops from the fierce African sun, resulting in severe sunburn, earning the British the mocking sobriquet 'rooinek' [red-necks], an insult which was sustained well into the twentieth century.

The second element of this idiom concerns the cultivated eccentricity of the British upper-classes. For example, Lord Rokeby had a fixation with water, spending so much time in the sea that on occasions he had to be dragged out of the water, unconscious. He built a large water tank at his home and spent considerable time floating in the water, eating his meals in the pool. His hair was uncut, reaching his waist, and was spread out on the surface of the tank as he lolled in the water.

How about Lord North? After marrying his American wife in the Caribbean in the autumn, he returned to England and told his wife he was going to bed. His wife was informed that Lord North stayed in bed between the 9th October and the 22nd March every year. North explained to his incredulous wife that this was a habit practiced by all the preceding Lords North since his ancestor, the prime minister Lord North, was defeated during the American War of Independence.

And then there was the obsessively shy fifth Duke of Portland, William John Cavendish Scott Bentick. So scared of human contact was Bentick that he lived underground in quarters connected by 15 miles of tunnels. One tunnel led to the railway station, where his blacked-out carriage was loaded on to the train. When he arrived in London his servants were banished from view, allowing him to enter his home without being seen.

Francis Henry Egerton was the dog-loving eighth Earl of Bridgewater. He ate at a large table accompanied by 12 dogs, each of which wore

So Noël Coward was not quite as original as we thought. His first performance of this song in 1931 was preceded by the wisdom of others. He didn't tell us that did he? However, the omission of ascription notwithstanding, no doubt he put this idiom on the map —look at the surge after 1931. Hats off to you, Noël.

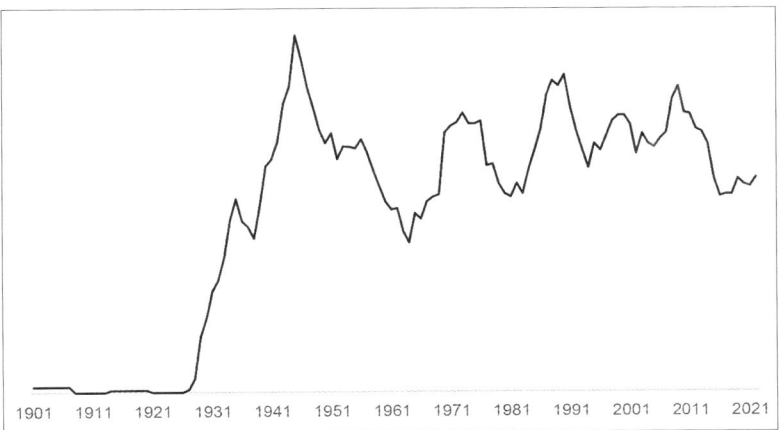

DOG AND BONE

WHAT ARE we without language? We can communicate by gesture, by touch and by a range of sounds; some even believe telepathically. But whilst these forms of communication helps us to bond together and share our needs, passions and pleasures, it is language and the ability this gives to cooperate which has enabled the human species to 'master' (and arguably also destroy) the bounty of nature. Of course other species need to communicate and also draw on a similar range of techniques. For example, chimpanzees and meerkats use a range of sounds to warn of different types of danger. A debate is raging amongst scientists about whether trees can communicate with each other through their underground microscopic fungal threads called mycorrhizal networks (the so-called 'wood wide web'). But no other species has developed languages which mirror the capacity of humans to communicate complex and nuanced ideas and feelings.

Spoken languages developed more than 100,000 years ago, probably in Africa during the Middle Stone Age. Inevitably, these spoken sounds developed special attributes to reflect the particular environment in which they developed. Similar human needs and emotions were articulated in different clusters of sounds, words and sentences and thus communication between people resulted in different languages (and accents and dialects). Even today, when so many have disappeared, the varied mountainous topography of New Guinea has led to an enormous diversity of languages. This country of less than eight million people has more than 1,000 languages and in some remote mountainous areas, people in one valley cannot understand those in an adjacent valley. War between these communities is often endemic.

Currently there are around 7,000 different spoken languages, and ninety per cent are spoken by less than 100,00 people. 46 languages are currently spoken by a single individual as the pressures of urbanisation and globalisation overwhelm the

This Book is NOT

local. Less than half of the 280 native American languages are still spoken, and the situation is even more dire in Australia where only 13 of the Aboriginal languages remain in daily use. UNESCO estimates that 2,500 languages are currently at threat from extinction globally and that a language is lost every three and a half months.

But if the survival of many languages is under threat, are there examples of languages which have been deliberately created? Since the 17th century, more than 200 artificial languages have been produced. Most of these resulted from the need to develop specialised ways of communicating technical ideas, such as in computer programming. Perhaps the most commendable example of language development was Esperanto, based on words and grammar of English, German, Latin and the Romance Languages. Esperanto—'one who hopes'—was created in Bialstok, Poland, in 1887 by Ludwig Zamenhof, a Jewish ophthalmologist. He believed that a common language would reduce the inter-communal tensions surfacing in anti-Semitic pogroms targeting the Jewish community (how wrong can you get...?). My father's family (he was born in Bialstock in 1906), was fluent in Esperanto, but that did not stop the Nazis murdering his parents and siblings during the war. Esperanto is still spoken by more than two million people worldwide.

Unlike Esperanto which was developed to facilitate and widen communication, sometimes new languages emerge so as to exclude people from communication. For example, as a child, my parents would sometimes converse in Yiddish to hide their exchanges. My wife and I were brought up in South Africa and learnt Afrikaans in our youth. When our children were young and when we didn't want them to know what we were saying, we would lapse into Afrikaans as a way of excluding them from our communication.

One way of excluding people from communication is to deliberately create a language which only a limited number of people can understand. This type of language is called 'slang', and slangs are generally spoken and not written. The more technical word for slang is argot, first recorded in 1628 in France to refer to a group of thieves, *les argotiers*, who developed a language to hide their nefarious intent.

Rhyming slang is a particular and often very complex type of slang. It uses a word or a phrase of two or more words as a substitute for a common word. But the distinctive feature of the rhyming step is that this phrase rhymes with the word it is replacing. So, as we will see below, the link between the phrase and the word it replaces is not obvious to outsiders, and is only recognised by those who are inside the 'slang gang'.

THE DOG IN COCKNEY RHYMING SLANG

A Cockney is a Londoner born within the sounds of the church bells of St. Mary-le-Bow in Cheapside. Before traffic drowned out these bells, it covered an area about six miles east, five miles north, four miles west, and three miles south of the church.

In 1822 Robert Peel established London's first professional police force. Soon after, Cockney rhyming slang developed, probably as a way of hiding communication from the police. It was also used for commercial advantage by street traders, exchanging information about customers and prices. It functions indirectly—one of the words in the slang phrase rhymes with the word which is being replaced. Over the centuries, Cockney rhyming slang evolved into a dialect of the English language. Increasingly is has become a tourist attraction, with a variety of Cockney slang dictionaries on sale. So here are some examples:

* *Going up 'the apples', means climbing the stairs. This is derived from 'apples and pears', as 'pairs' rhymes with 'stairs'*
* *'Wife' means trouble, because of course a wife is associated with trouble and 'strife'*
* *Often, the rhyming slang is not limited to a single word and a two to three word phrase is used instead. For example, 'use your loaf', refers to using your head, that is thinking about what you are doing. 'Loaf' is linked to a 'loaf of bread' and 'bread' rhymes with 'head'.*

- *Some slang has become a little more roundabout. 'Taking the mickey' was originally Mickey Bliss, the rhyming slang of 'taking the piss', British slang for ridiculing someone. Similarly, 'telling porkies' is derived from 'pork pies', which rhymes with 'lies'.*
- *In many cases, Cockney slang developed to avoid using swearwords. 'Berk' (a foolish person) refers to the famous Berkeley Hunt fox-hunt, which rhymes with 'cunt'. 'Cobblers' (you are talking rubbish) comes from cobblers awls, which rhymes with balls (testicles). And 'ampton' is a shortened form of Hampton, which in turn is a shortening of Hampton Wick, a place in London, which rhymes with 'prick', referring to someone you don't like. 'Pony and trap' rhymes with 'crap' (nonsense) and blowing a 'raspberry' (a rude sound of derision) derives from raspberry tart, which rhymes with 'fart'.*
- *British university students distinguish their examination results with a Geoff Hurst (famous footballer) (a first class pass), Attila the Hun an upper second (2:1, two-point-one), a Desmond Tutu (lower second, 2:2, two-point-two) and a Thora Hird (Douglas Hurd, a British politician of the 1990s).*

In the Encyclopaedia Britannica, Adam Jacot de Bonoid illustrates Cockney rhyming slang with a string linked to celebrities

I left my Claire Rayners [trainers] down the Fatboy Slim [gym] so I was late for the Basil Fawlty [balti, a type of curry]. The Andy McNab [cab] cost me an Ayrton Senna [a 'tenner,' or £10 note], but it didn't stop me getting the Britney Spears [beers] in. Next thing you know it turned into a Gary Player [all-dayer] and I was off my Chevy Chase ['off my face', or drunk].

But what about the dog in the story of Cockney rhyming slang? Its obvious really. What rhymes with a phone (= telephone)? A bone of course. And what is always associated with a bone? A dog of course. So a 'dog and bone', or sometimes just a 'dog', is clearly a phone. Obvious, innit?

*Raphie Kaplinsky, Development Economist (Retired)
and Jeremy Jones, Dog Walker.
Barcombe Mills and Burgess Hill, UK.*

Citations of Dog and Bone rise after the 1980s. Perhaps after the tourist boom hits London, or that we don't want people to know that we are speaking on the dog and bone. On the other hand, the fall in citations after 2013 suggests that dog and bone refers to a fixed line phone and not a mobile phone.

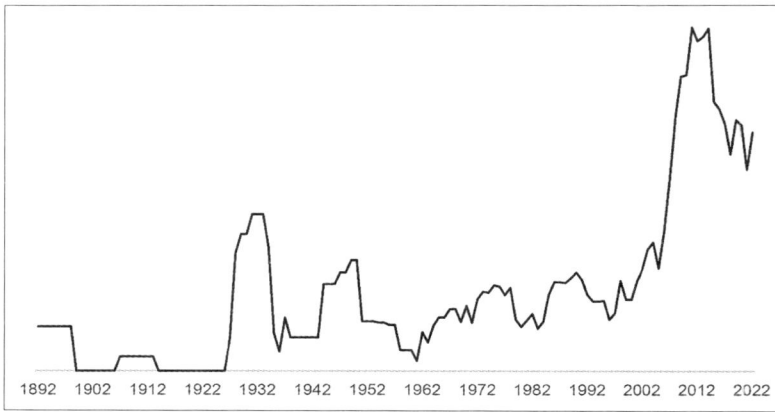

This Book is NOT

LET SLEEPING DOGS LIE

HAVE YOU ever been woken from deep sleep in the middle of the night by your partner, a parent, a friend or perhaps an intruder? And if so, you were irritated, right? And you snapped at the offender, right? So its not just dogs who should be left alone when they are taking a nap. And beware—if you waken someone from their slumbers, you might well get an earful, or worse. And however strident the reaction from your partner, parent or friend may be, the response of a disturbed dog—perhaps a Rottweiler—might be a little more troublesome.

There is a nuance to this metaphor. On the one hand, it is just telling you to take care when you tread on sensitive ground, when you might inadvertently expose suppressed feelings and find yourself on the other side of a mouthful. But on the other hand it also offers a stronger admonition. Do not stir trouble in circumstances when you know the results might be more than you bargained for. And this applies not just to meddling in other people's business at a personal level, but in the wider realm of geo-politics too. For example, in 1870 the *New York Times* commented on Britain's experience in the Crimean War:

> Let us consider why Russia has gained enough to suppose she is sufficiently strong to infringe the wholesome rule to 'let sleeping dogs lie' when applied to the English. The Crimean War showed her plainly that her people were barbarians, and that her strength lay in brute force.

The danger of inadvertently stirring up trouble—either through carelessness or as a result of deliberate intervention—is of course central to all human interactions. It is not surprising therefore that the bible engaged with the issue, although not literally in terms of waking a sleeping dog—'He that passes by, and meddles with strife belonging not to him, is like one that takes a dog by the ears' (*Book of Proverbs*, 26:17). The idiom is found in French in the early 14th century, with the saying *'Ne reveillez pas le chien qui dort'* (Do not wake the dog that sleeps) and was used by Chaucer in 1374 in *Troilus and Criseyde* ('It is nought good a sleepyng hound to wake). A collection of proverbs in 1546 by John Heywood includes the idiom 'It is euill [evil] wakying of the slepyng dog'. Although the English prime minister Robert Walpole is frequently cited as using this idiom during the 18th century, there is no written record of him doing so. The idiom became more popular in the 19th century. For example, in *David Copperfield*, Charles Dickens writes 'Let sleeping dogs lie—who wants to rouse 'em?'.

LET SLEEPING DOGS LIE

I went up to Cambridge in September 2020, in the middle of the Covid pandemic and after a summer of isolated relaxation, following the complete cancellation of all my school-leaving exams and a hair-raising wait for predicted grades as results. All lectures, supervisions and seminars were online. I didn't meet my director of studies or tutor in person until after Easter 2021. I moved in knowing that the 12 people in my corridor 'bubble' were my prescribed group of friends, with little opportunity for the spreading of one's wings or making the city one's own. I was lucky. Karisma, the girl who would become my long-term partner moved in next to me. So while the prospects of a large social circle were, for the moment, limited, I at least found a different kind of excitement and sense of growing up.

That September was a limbo period between the first absolute lockdown and the less draconian January lockdown when you were allowed to meet in a group of six, but pubs had to close by 10pm. The clubs were open for sit-down events, but, of course, only until 10pm. You would queue outside at 6pm wearing masks, embarrassed as commuters cycled by while you sipped your pre-drinks. Inside, you had to sit at your designated table of six, struggling to talk given the too-loud music but forbidden from dancing or singing (the DJ would turn the volume down and talk over the choruses). These events gave us a semblance of a 'fresher' experience and a place where you could cement friendships in person, socialising in the way university students tend to.

Covid forced Cambridge to transfer its student support structure into a system of policing. The college porters tracked where we scanned our keycards, watched us on CCTV and patrolled constantly. We had a system of weekly household mandatory PCR testing, so Covid was quickly discovered. The age-old tension between students and the institution in power was tempered by a respect for the pandemic and a founded fear of the consequences of breaking the rules; both from a sense of social responsibility but also a personal worry about the reality of spending 14 days in isolation in a university room, if you, or someone in your household, were to get Covid.

When I inevitably had to isolate, my household was allocated a gazebo in the garden and, like prisoners, we were allowed an hourly slot to spend outside. We would take our laptops and sit awkwardly, trying to maximise our breaths of fresh air before returning to our rooms.

People did, of course, have parties and colleges varied in the strictness of their policing regimes. But the disapproval of one's house mates and the fear of academic repercussions if you were caught (particularly for the medics who faced a fitness-for-practice warning) led to a strained environment of guilt and emotional confusion that inhibited rule-breaking.

Over Christmas, a resurgence of the virus led to a strict winter lockdown. Cambridge told us not to come back after the holidays, to do the term online from home. However, a combination of Wi-Fi problems and my college being more lenient than most left me one of the few who were allowed to come back. It was a term of eerie quiet with empty corridors. We cooked, went for walks, and got drunk together in our rooms.

On the morning of my partner's 19th birthday, we were woken by a phone call telling us we had tested positive on the university PCR testing system. Stress. We were confident that this was a false positive—we had all tested positive the previous term and knew that the university testing often picked up on previous virus and presented a false positive result. Moreover, none of us had symptoms and we were negative on lateral flows.

I am not proud of what happened that evening. A friend from a different household had made Karisma a birthday cake and so we blocked open the door at one end of the corridor and sat two metres apart on either side of the door to have cake and a short celebration. Unluckily, we were seen by a porter and awoke the next day to that dreaded email from the college dean of discipline who had the power to fine us or evict us from our accommodation. In the subsequent zoom disciplinary meeting my flatmates and I perched nervously on one laptop, prepared to tell her the truth. But she just didn't seem to hear what we were saying and instead spun a completely alternative narrative. When I said 'we opened the door to receive a cake', she fed back 'ah yes, you opened the door because you needed more space because you were feeling claustrophobic in your corridor'. Odd. We didn't know how to respond but to agree. Yes, we replied, gingerly, 'we had been claustrophobic'. The conversation ended with us apologising and her saying she understood. Later that day, our secondary

This Book is NOT

One of the key contributions made by the psychoanalysts Sigmund Freud and Carl Jung to our understanding of how our minds function was the idea of the 'unconscious', which often results in us inadvertently blurting out troubling thoughts without prior thought. They thought that the unravelling of the unconscious was a healing process so would certainly not have subscribed to the idea that we should always let sleeping dogs lie. Does the fact that Freud and Jung developed these ideas in the early 20th century and that psychoanalysis became increasingly popular in the last decades of the century explain the uptick in citations after the turn of the millennium?

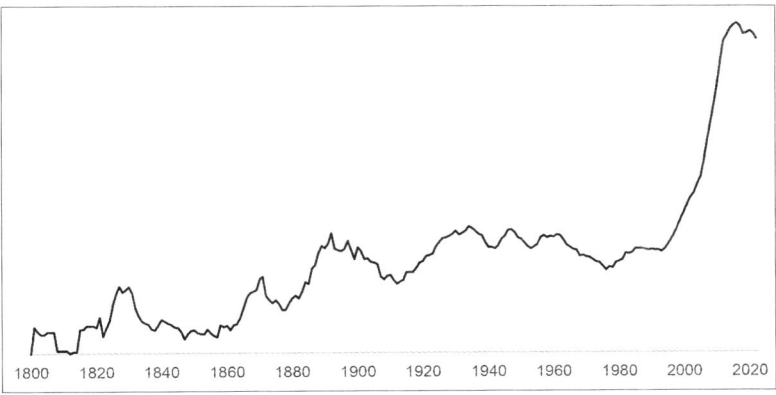

THE QUICK BROWN FOX JUMPS OVER THE LAZY DOG

THE QUICK brown fox jumps over the lazy dog is a widely used English pangram. A pangram is a sentence which incorporates every letter of the alphabet, in this idiom, achieving the objective with a sentence of 35 letters. There are shorter pangrams but none of these make sense, for example *Waltz, bad nymph, for quick jigs vex* (28 letters), *Glib jocks quiz nymph to vex dwarf* (28 letters) and *Sphinx of black quartz, judge my vow.* An anagram is a pangram which only uses each alphabetical letter once, such as *Mr Jock, TV quiz PhD, bags few lynx.*

The earliest reference to this idiom was in the *Boston Journal* in 1885, although it used the form 'A quick' rather than 'The quick'. It was offered as an aide to teachers to assist students learning to write. The typewriter was patented in 1868 and was first sold commercially in 1874 in the US. By the 1880s typewriters were widely used in offices and the pangram *The quick brown fox jumped over the lazy dog* was widely employed to speed up the productivity of the first typists. As a productivity aid it rapidly trumped the widely-used alternative *now is the time for all good men to come to the aid of the party* (49 letters), although arguably the longer pangram was of more use to society. In 1908 Baden-Powell, the founder of the Scouts movement, used the anagram to teach signalling skills to young boys in *Scouting for Boys*, accompanied by this illustration

One of the more exotic uses of this mundane anagram was during the Cuban Missile Crisis in 1963 when the world was frighteningly close to a catastrophic global nuclear conflict. In an attempt to prevent the accidental triggering of war, the American and Russian governments agreed to the installation of a direct telephonic hotline

This Book is NOT

between Presidents Kennedy and Khrushchev. The American side tested the system with a slightly elongated version of the idiom— The quick brown fox jumped over the lazy dog's back 1234567890. The Russians responded quizzically 'What does it mean when your people say "The quick brown fox jumped over the lazy dog?"'

The idiom is currently used in the annual Zaner-Bloser National Handwriting Competition in the US. Microsoft also employs it to test computer typefaces—try typing =rand()in Office Word 2003 and =rand.old() in Office Word 2007.

BEYOND ENGLISH

Is there an equivalent to The quick brown fox jumps over the lazy dog in other languages? Yes, but it's a little complicated, since some languages use inflexions such as ç, ä, and š. It is even more complicated in character-languages such as Chinese which has more than 20,000 characters. As an aid to calligraphy teachers, in the 6th century, Emperor Wu commissioned the writing of the Thousand Character Classic poem. It consisted of exactly one thousand characters each used only once, grouped into 250 four-line rhyming stanzas.

Pangrams used in their shortest forms in a range of languages:

Bulgarian:
Фучейки и хълцайки, кьоравият грухтящ шопар жадно стъпка зюмбюлите
Snorting and whimpering, the grunting blind boar hungrily trampled the hyacinths.

Czech
Nechť již hříšné saxofony ďáblů rozezvučí síň úděsnými tóny waltzu, tanga a quickstepu.
Let the sinful saxophones of devils finally make the hall resonate with the frightful tones of waltz, tango and quickstep

---

Danish—an Anagram!

> *Høj bly gom vandt fræk sexquiz på wc*
> *Tall shy groom won dirty sex quiz on WC*

Finish

> *Charles Darwin jammaili Åken hevixylofonilla Qatarin yöpub*
> *Zeligissä.*
> *Charles Darwin was jamming on Åke's heavy metal xylophone in*
> *the Qatar night pub Zelig.*

West Frisian

> *Alve bazige froulju wachtsje op dyn komst*
> *Eleven bossy women await your arrival*

French

> *Buvez de ce whisky que le patron juge fameux. (36)*
> *Drink some of this whisky which the boss finds excellent.*

Greek

> διαφυλάξτε γενικά τη ζωή σας από βαθειά ψυχικά τραύματα
> *Protect in general your life from deep psychological wounds*

Hebrew (Anagram)

> ידו, הסח מעטב רזג תצק לכא ופש
> *A rabbit ate some lettuce flavoured carrot and that's it*

Icelandic (Anagram)

> *Kæmi ný öxi hér, ykist þjófum nú bæði víl og ádrepa.*
> *If a new axe were here, thieves would feel increasing deterrence and*
> *punishment*

This Book is NOT

Irish

D'fuascail Íosa Úrṁac na hÓiġe Beannaiṫe pór Éaḃa agus Áḋaiṁ

Jesus, Son of the blessed Virgin, redeemed the seed of Eve and Adam.

Italian

Quel vituperabile xenofobo zelante assaggia il whisky ed esclama: alleluja!

That blameworthy, zealous xenophobe tastes his whisky and exclaims: Alleluja!

Korean

Kiseu-ui goyujogeoneun ipsulkkiri mannaya hago teukbyeolhan gisureun pilyochi antha

The essential condition for a kiss is that lips meet and there is no special technique required.

Polish

Koń i żółw grali w kości z piękną ćmą u źródła.

A horse and a tortoise played dice with a beautiful moth near the spring.

Romanian

Bând whisky, jazologul șprițuit vomă fix în tequila.

Drinking whisky, the drunken jazzman threw up right in the tequila.

Russian

Широкая электрификация южных губерний даст мощный толчок подъёму сельского хозяйства.

Widespread electrification of southern Guberniyas [a local district in pre-Soviet Russia] will give a powerful incentive to the rise of agriculture.

And, finally, a pangram made up of recognised two-letter country codes:
BD, CV, ET, FR, HN, IL, JP, KG, MX, QA, SO, UY, ZW
(Bangladesh, Cape Verde, Ethiopia, France, Honduras, Israel,
Japan, Kyrgyzstan, Mexico, Qatar, Somalia, Uruguay and
Zimbabwe)

Raphie Kaplinsky, Development Economist (Retired)
Barcombe Mills, UK.

Was the jump in citations to this idiom between 2005 and 2008 a result of more people learning to touch-type so that they could put their CVs and family-histories on the internet? Or perhaps the sharp rise jump in references between 2005 and 2009 actually was a quick brown fox jumping over a lazy dog? It certainly looks like it.

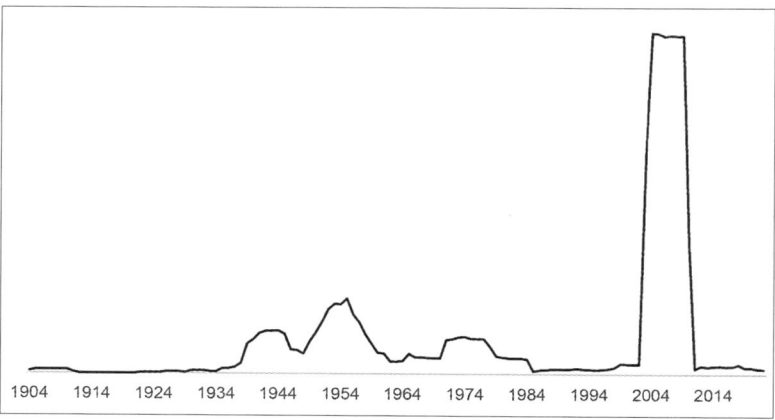

This Book is NOT

LIKE A DOG WITH TWO TAILS

IF SOMEONE says you are like a dog with two tails, you are not only pleased, happy or proud with something, but you are unusually pleased, happy or proud. The word 'delight' comes to mind, and the image which it sparks is of an adorable puppy wildly excited by a ball, a treat, a find or an owner returning after an absence.

This idiom is often believed to have been of North American origin, but in fact the first recorded use was in a poem by John Gay during the early 18th century. (Gay was the author of the famous *Beggar's Opera*, which satirically lampooned the English upper classes for their fawning devotion to Italian operas). The poem, *The Dog's Shadow*, includes the following lines:

> How covetous is man! (the Dog reply'd)
> Had I been satisfi'd with what I had,
> This double Portion might have still been mine;
> But now I've lost my own, by seeking more,
> And am, like you, a Dog without a Bone,
> Or, what is worse, a Dog with two Tails.

Gay probably drew on one of Aesop's fables which were collected in the 6th century BC. It tells a story of a dog who discovers a piece of meat, runs away, and then sees his reflection in the water. Thinking it is a dog with a bigger portion of meat, the dog drops his find in the hope of seizing the larger piece of meat, and loses it. This message of this fable was to warn about the danger of greed, with Gray adding the embellishment of a dog with two tails.

The idiom has evolved over time. It no longer warns us about the danger of greed, but instead has morphed into a metaphor of extreme delight. Pascal Tréguer, a French citizen residing in Britain who specialises in the uncovering the history of words and phrases, traced an early reference to this idiom in a letter from Zebulan Harrowtooth, in Boston, to his uncle, Jonathan Hoehandle, in Vermont. It was published in the *Western Herald & Steubenville Gazette* in Ohio in 1822 and contained the line 'he swaggers like a dog with two tails'. The assiduous Tréguer records its further use in a letter to the *Edwardsville Spectator* by Simon Snorer in 1826. The idiom was famously used by Tom Taylor in his play *Our American Cousin*, which contained the line 'I'm as happy as a dog with two tails, and I don't care who knows it'. (Taylor was obviously a dog-lover; the play also contained the line 'Like the tail wagging the dog'). The 'fame' of Taylor's play arises from the fact that it was the play that Abraham Lincoln was watching in the Ford's Theatre in Washington when he was assassinated by John Wilkes Booth in 1865.

So much for the changed meaning of this idiom and its widespread use to reflect feelings of delight and great happiness. But can dogs really have two tails? The answer is that this does sometimes happen, albeit very rarely. In February 2021 a dog was born in Oklahoma with six legs and two tails (and 2 pelvic regions, 2 lower urinary tracts, 2 reproductive systems). This deformity was a result of a rare disorder named monocephalus dipygus. The same phenomenon has also been observed in a goat. In 2019 a puppy was born in Missouri with a second leg growing out of its forehead. We do not know how any of these unfortunate animals fared as they grew older.

LURKING IN THE BUSHES…

I didn't see the photographer lurking in the bushes as I walked my dogs that morning, but the mounted police officer did. I remember him well as he trotted over on his horse to speak to me. Molly and Benson, my Tibetan Terriers, snuffled around, happy to be out exploring undergrowth, their tails curling cutely over their backs as they sniffed out a world of familiar and unfamiliar smells.

I was six months pregnant, and I don't mind saying, it was a hard time. Three earlier pregnancies had ended in miscarriage. But things seemed on track this time, and walking the dogs near my home in West London was a daily delight—for them and for me.

I was regularly presenting the BBC's Six o'Clock News at the time, and the officer had recognised me. His greeting was friendly but serious. He hadn't come to exchange pleasantries. He wanted to warn me that he'd seen a long lens lurking in the undergrowth, trained on me and the dogs: paparazzi.

Suddenly, the carefree walk in the park took an unpleasant turn. Not again. It wasn't the first time the tabloid press had taken an unwelcome interest in my frankly mundane days. They'd snapped me on my honeymoon four years before. They has also routinely trawled through the garbage cans outside our house ('Oh, it wasn't a fox').

I've found out since that some 'celebs' let it be known where they'll be at a certain time rather than risk having unsupervised photographs slip into the gossip pages. Not me. I've never sought out the attention of the paparazzi—quite the reverse. I value my family's privacy far too much. Let others make their pacts with the devil.

Besides, I can't see why anyone would be interested in taking a long-lens photo of a heavily pregnant woman walking in a park, except that I know from bitter experience the cunning ways of the media pack: if they thought their sneaked shots might find a buyer on a Fleet Street newsdesk… well then, it was easy money.

'Woman walks dogs' isn't much of a story on even the slowest news day. But that's what the pictures must have shown. A woman, some trees, a police officer and two dogs. I imagine the picture editor looking at the photos being offered for sale and getting on the phone to the snapper:

Picture editor: 'What's the story here, then? Looks like she's just taking her dogs for a walk.'
Photographer: 'Yeah, but a copper went over and spoke to her.'
Picture editor: 'I can see that, but what did he say?'
Photographer: 'I dunno, but he looked really cross.'
Picture editor: 'What, with her?'
Photographer: 'Well I don't know, but who else can it have been?'
Picture editor: 'OK—don't worry. We'll sort something out. Now, I need you to go to High Barnet quickly—Tess Daly's been spotted in Sainsbury's.

This Book is NOT

I'll never know what happened in that newsroom that day. What I do know is that the next morning's Daily Vile carried a snatched photograph of me talking to that charming policeman with my little dogs. It was only then that what had happened in the park became clear to me. I had, the paper gleefully reported, received a fine for not clearing up after my dog. It was pure, cynical fabrication They must have calculated that the chances of my bothering to complain were small and if they were forced to carry a correction, they could hide it in two tiny lines at the bottom of p17. That snapper will have been paid for his furtive pictures. He must have been delighted with his day's work. Like a dog with two tails.

Natasha Kaplinsky, Journalist, TV Presenter,
Winner Strictly Come Dancing

References to this idiom tell us little except that there was a spurt around the time of Abraham Lincoln's assassination in 1865 (could Taylor's play have been that influential?) and after the global financial crisis in the early 2000s. Perhaps the most recent spurt is a reflection of the glee experienced by the very wealthy who have benefitted disproportionately as so many in the rest of the world have fallen into destitution and become victims of the rapidly unfolding environmental crisis?

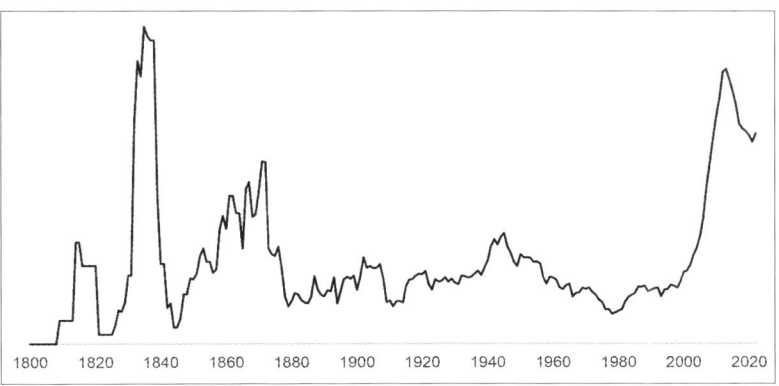

DOGGED

OVER THE past millennium, an increasing number of the world's population has been freed from the need to grow and forage their own food and protect themselves from wild animals and rodents. Coinciding with this shift from countryside to town and from agriculture to industry, has been a change in the relationship between humans and domesticated animals. Dogs and cats increasingly morphed from servants (guards and rodent hunters) to friends and family. And just as our relationship with animals has changed over the centuries, so has the meaning of the idiom 'dogged'.

During the latter years of the Middle English period (1250-1500) there are records of people being described as doggid or Doggyd to reflect the fact that they were mean, surly, contemptible or cruelly malicious. By the late 18th century dogged had assumed a somewhat different and less negative meaning, implying a person or animal who was silently obstinate. Although less negative than cruel or malicious, silent obstinacy is hardly a phrase of endearment. But as the relationship between humans and dogs became more familial and intimate, the word dogged shifted from a negative connotation to an admiring one. Nowadays, to say that someone or some animal is dogged implies that their behaviour is characterised by admirable persistence and resilience. It describes the determined and tenacious ability to withstand adverse conditions. If you are dogged you cannot rely on luck, or be hampered by fate or destiny. You make your own luck. In the words of the golfer Gary Player, 'the more I practice, the luckier I get'.

This Book is NOT

DOGGED BY SUCCESS AND AMBITION

To say that one pursues a goal with doggedness does not necessarily imply that the pursuit is likely to succeed, nor that it should. Dogs themselves reveal this fact of doggedness: some never learn to reliably retrieve a thrown ball, however doggedly their human companions attempt to train them, while others doggedly return a ball when you might wearily wish for a break.

Take, for instance, the pointer named Chase, late of our family, who was so relentless a retriever of pitched objects that he would drop a ball onto a pile of leaves being raked, say, or into a hole being dug for transplanting, then, as soon as the ball was tossed, would rush off to retrieve it again, leaving but a moment for the human to transact anything before the next pitch was demanded. Over and over this would happen, until raking or transplanting would be abandoned—dogs being more dogged than humans, at least in our family.

This attribute reached its embarrassing apogee when painters were at work on our home, and Chase deposited his ball into a five gallon can of aubergine soft gloss acrylic paint. Doggedness can be annoying.

Or it may be an attribute of genius. Charles Darwin reported being ill just about every day of the five years he spent on the voyage of the HMS Beagle, but he nevertheless returned to England with voluminous notes, specimens and sketches that guided his work for years ahead. Darwin never fully regained his health, but he doggedly pursued observations and note-taking. Indeed, Darwin himself cites relentlessness as a key factor leading to his scientific accomplishment. 'My industry has been nearly as great as it could have been in the observation and collection of facts', he wrote in his autobiography. That single-minded determination enabled him to overcome a lifetime of maladies, he noted, because it 'makes me for the time forget, or drives quite away, my daily discomfort'.

Darwin was 29 when the Beagle returned to England, but he kept at the hour-by-hour work the voyage had inspired—observation, cogitation, note-taking, synthesis and writing—until he felt ready, finally, at age 50, to publish On the Origin of Species. *By a dozen or so years later, most of England's scientific community had accepted his theory of evolution,* but it wasn't until several decades after his death that a broad global consensus emerged that natural selection was, indeed, the basic method of evolution. Today we recognize evolution as the unifying theory of the life sciences, as Darwin had doggedly believed.

While few people have the impact of Charles Darwin, there are many examples of people doggedly keeping at their work and finding success late in life. Harland Sanders, for example, was 40 when he first started serving fried chicken at a restaurant alongside his gas station in Kentucky, and 62 when he first franchised the recipe to another restaurant. Even after that, Sanders' restaurants came and went, but he remained sure that his recipe for pressure-frying chicken could be successful. It wasn't until he was 73 that Sanders trademarked the phrase, 'It's Finger Lickin' Good', and launched the explosion of Kentucky Fried Chicken (KFC) into a global fast-food phenomenon.

But while success late in life may sometimes be attributed to doggedness, early achievement may yield less laudable examples of doggedness as a habit. Perhaps none is more notable than that of the American politician Harold Stassen. His rise was meteoric: Stassen was elected governor of Minnesota in 1938, when he was just 31 years old, and was twice re-elected by huge margins. The acclaim seemingly enflamed Stassen's ambitions, and he vigorously vied for the Republican presidential nomination in both 1944 and 1948, narrowly losing both times at the party's nominating conventions to the New York governor, Thomas E. Dewey. Thereafter, no amount of dogged campaigning brought Stassen success. He continued to seek the presidency—in 1952, 1964, 1968, 1980, 1984, 1988 and 1992— winning, in the process, only the notoriety of a perennial loser. Undaunted, he also ran for governor of Minnesota again, for a Minnesota U.S. Senate seat (twice), for governor of Pennsylvania (twice), for a seat in the U.S. House of Representatives and for mayor of Philadelphia.

Doggedness, then, is neither a guarantee of success nor necessarily an admirable trait. Just as there are dogs to admire and dogs to avoid, the attribute of doggedness depends much upon the individual.

Reg Smith, Newspaper Editor (Retired)
New York State, USA.

This Book is NOT

Curiously, the citations to dogged seem to fall during periods of economic depression—the 1830s, the 1870s, the 1930s and after 2008. Try and make sense of that! Perhaps if we concentrate on writing books containing the idiom dogged we will be able to emerge from the economic slump which has dogged us since 2008.

GOING TO THE DOGS

L IKE ALMOST all idioms, 'going to the dogs' has more than one meaning and its origins are obscure. The most common meaning refers to something in the world around us which has been created by humans and which has seen better days. How suitable for contemporary Britain. Our National Health Service, formerly setting the highest global standards for civilised healthcare, is in disarray as are the post-privatised water-, postal- and transport utilities. Used in this way, the idiom lays a finger of blame—the relevant powers, in this case the government, have wilfully allowed, or indeed driven, the service to decay. There is however also a less blameful meaning of the idiom when it is used to observe a process of gradual decline as a consequence of oversight or negligence—a garden, once luxuriant and well-tended has been neglected and has become overgrown with weeds.

However, in recent years the phrase has also come to assume a completely different meaning. Greyhound dog-racing has become a popular sport and is the sixth most popular sport in Britain. More than four million people a year go to the dogs and bet on the results of a series of races involving misshapen dogs 'haring' after a mechanical 'rabbit'. In this sense, the idiom going to the dogs has seen a reversal of its negative meaning. Instead of referring to a sense of despair and collapse, it describes a world of abandonment and fun. The novelist Alexandra Fuller writes about her troubled childhood in colonial Rhodesia and Malawi. She wishes that her parents would have been more caring and attentive instead of pursuing a life of hedonism. Her autobiography is entitled *Don't Let's Go to the Dogs Tonight*.

Groucho Marx quipped enigmatically '*Where shall we go tonight? I don't know about you, but I'm going to the dogs*'. Did he mean he was out for fun (like Alexandra Fuller's parents), or was he on a journey of disrepair? (Talking about Groucho and dogs, he also said '*Outside of a dog, a book is a man's best friend. Inside of a dog, it's too dark to read*').

There are common but unrelated origins to this idiom. Both in China and in medieval Europe, many cities were walled for protection against intruders. In these relatively early years of interaction between humans and dogs, the dogs were left to roam wild beyond the city-walls, often baying with hunger or fighting over territory and sexual partners. People who were expelled as outcasts from the city would be exiled outside the city-walls—they would be sent to the dogs. A less-likely origin of the idiom is traced back to a similar era in 18th century Britain where an unsuccessful hunting party would be characterised as gone to the dogs, describing a hunt where the dogs had failed in their task of locating the prey.

At about this time the idiom began to enter the literary world. A play entitled *Germanicus, A Tragedy* was performed in London in 1775 and used the idiom to reflect a world of decay and degradation:

Sirrah, they are prostitutes, and are civil to delude and destroy you; they are painted Jezebels, and they who hearken to 'em, like Jezebel of old, will go to the dogs; if you dare to look at 'em, you will be tainted, and if you speak to 'em you are undone.

In 1816, *The Memoirs of the late Thomas Holcroft*, included the pitiful observation 'A rascal, who is a known sharper in these parts, hearing of the aversion I had to cruelty, bought an old, one-eyed horse, that was going to the dogs, for five shillings'.

And in 1917, in *Augustus does his Bit*, George Bernard Shaw concludes that 'The country is going to the dogs'.

THE DAY I WENT TO THE DOGS

Its on rare occasions these days that I catch the aroma of wet tweed coats, the whiff, the passing glance of the smell of real tobacco always accompanied by that cheerful but raucous cough, and when I do I am transported back to the night in August 1952, going to the dogs at the track in Clonmel, County Tipperary.

I was left to be minded by my young aunt and her husband. Their notion of child care was never to sit at home, but to take me wherever they were going. This involved trips to their work, expeditions to country pubs, falling asleep in late night cinema and going racing, horses and dogs.

That special evening, I was pulled through the crowd, local farmers, local shop keepers, my head at elbow height which involving ducking and wriggling, while above I heard the cheerful comments, 'See you are minding The Child again, she'll bring you luck tonight' and then there we were right against the rails of the parade ring as the athletes were led in.

Led by white coated kennel staff, the tall, long, lean multicoloured hounds, gazed upon the crowd with disdain, but with keen anticipation, while a small crowd gathered around my uncle, trying to see what dogs he had marked on his card, what tips he muttered to a favoured few. My aunt said to me,

This Book is NOT

'Which one will it be?' (aunt)

'Chancer' (me)

'Chancer, he's running track 4, he loves track 4' (aunt)

'Chancer, that old butcher's dog. You know sometimes he never even leaves that starting gate, just sits there looking at all the others chasing off' (aunt)

'But there are days he runs and he looked at me and gave me a wink, he'll win' (me)

We met up with my uncle at the long line of bookies, the only ones, it was said, guaranteed to go home with more money than when they arrived. Bundles of bank notes were passed over, a bet made in low tones, in return of a ticket carefully stored in a top pocket.

'Has she chosen?'

'God help us the child is cracked, it's only The Chancer she's picked out.'

Even the bookie laughed, 'Shouldn't really take your money, but I'll give you 500 to 1 on Bengurrah Boy the butcher's dog'.

'That's his racing name, but I prefer Chancer' I said and handed over my sticky warm pound as the people around laughed, calling to the bookie,

'Don't spend the child's money on a pint, you should give it to charity.'

My aunt smiled, 'Well in that case I'll put a quid on too, its a fun way of giving to the orphans'. But turning to my uncle muttered, 'Old Chancer, if he does decide to race he could well win', and he too placed a pound. The dogs came onto the racing track. One or two started to speak, hounds don't bark. Were they sorting out the finishing order between themselves?

The dogs were shoved in the starting boxes, the mechanical hare swung around the track, and just as it passed, six gates flew open and six dogs soared out in one magnificent leap, the pack intent on the kill, each dog focused on the prey. A gasp from the crowd, 'He started, he's second'. Pencils were taken out from behind ears, marks made in notebooks. The dogs rounded the last corner, some knocking and shoving but one focused, just ahead. Over the finish line the hare was stopped, leapt upon, teeth gnawing the leather, kennel staff ran out to haul the dogs away before a serious fight could start.

And yes dear reader, as you may have guessed it was my wonderful Chancer aka Bengurrah Boy that won and yet I cannot recall what happened later that evening, how my aunt and uncle broke the news to my austere parents that they'd taken me to the dogs, how they accounted for a boost to their savings. But sadly I never was allowed to stay with them again. What I did learn was that old Chancer, to the end of his long life, never was entered a race again, was never kept in outside kennels, but sat before a warm fire eating the very best that his butcher owner could provide and surrounded by photos of the day he won, proving the wise Irish saying, 'If you bring a greyhound into your house, you say hello to the dog and good bye to your couch'.

Rosalyn St Pierre, Lecturer and
Elected County Councillor (Retired), Barcombe, UK.

Going to the Dogs? The Second World War seems to have sobered us up, although we did seem to lose our discipline around the turn of the millennium. We sobered up again after that but will we hold our resolution during the turmoil of the 2020s? After all, what better way do we have of coping with global warming than slipping out for a tipple?

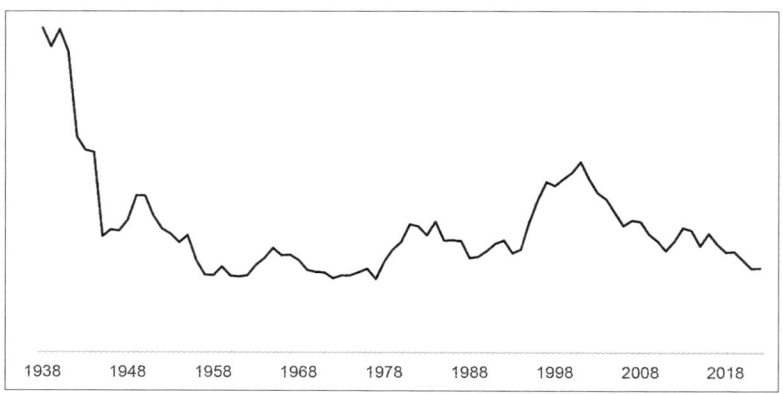

This Book is NOT

EYE OF NEWT AND TOE OF FROG, WOOL OF BAT AND TONGUE OF DOG

THE PSYCHOANALYST Carl Jung helped us to recognise how our everyday fears and behaviour can be understood through hidden archetypal characteristics in our psyches such as 'the shadow, the collective unconscious, the archetype and synchronicity'. In today's western society we have come to draw on these hidden archetypes to help our personal development and shape how we join with others in society. But, long before Jung developed his theories in the early twentieth century, and not just in Switzerland, the hidden forces of 'magic' have played a critical role in shaping the way in which people in all human societies understand the world around them. 'Magic' represents something which is mysterious, either because events cannot be explained by current knowledge and belief systems, or because there is a wish for a different outcome to that which is foreshadowed by existing events.

The way psychoanalysis provides insights into the 'unseen' unconscious world is in many ways similar to the role played by white witches in virtually all human societies. White witches use magic for selfless purposes, customarily through the mediums of blessings, incantations, charms, prayers and songs. In contrast, black witchcraft involves the use of magic for malign or evil purposes, often foretelling doom or providing incantations or potions to harm unsuspecting persons or to wreak revenge. (Do you need to be told that these colour-associations emanate from European rather than African culture?). We approve of white witchcraft. But we fear black witchcraft.

Anthropologists have documented the benign and malign use of magic across the world. For example the anthropologist Monica Wilson lived with the Nyakyusa peoples in Tanzania and Malawi. The BaNyakyusa would understand that the person who was killed by a falling coconut had suffered a severe head-injury. But, they would then ask, 'Why had that coconut fallen at precisely that time and at that spot, and who caused this to happen?' In the same Nyakyusa community, traditional healers used local herbs to treat a range of illnesses, including those which western medicines could not heal. They also used herbs and incantations to deal with neurotic and psychotic phobias and fears.

Belief in black and white magic continue to exist in modern western societies. Satanism—black magic—continues to thrive in the USA and Europe. In May 2023 the world's largest gathering of anti-religious Satanists met at a convention in the Little Black Chapel at the Marriott Hotel in Boston, USA. And if you check the internet, healers and seers (white witches) are living near you and will provide solace and predict your future. Astrologists will even tell you who you will marry and how many children you will have. So the belief in the power of magic to throw light on the unseen and to shape the world thrives in rich and poor countries alike.

Accusations of witchcraft—notably the use of black magic— were very common in England prior to the Witchcraft Act of 1735. Between 1400 and 1775, about 100,000 people were prosecuted for witchcraft in Europe and America and between 40,000 and 60,000 were executed. They were either burnt at the stake or thrown into a lake—if she floated, it was deemed that she was in league with the devil, rejecting the baptismal water. If she sank, she was 'cleared. And dead!' Around 80% of convicted witches were women, generally older women. The Witchcraft Act of 1735 made it illegal to accuse anyone of a crime of witchcraft in the UK and in 1727 Janet Horne was the last person to be executed for witchcraft in Great Britain.

Shakespeare wrote *Macbeth* in 1606, during the height of belief in witchcraft. In one of the most famous scenes in all of his plays, he gives us three witches concocting a brew for Macbeth, the Thane (a nobleman) of Glamis and a brave general in King Duncan's army. The spell they cast is as follows:

> Eye of newt, and toe of frog,
> Wool of bat, and tongue of dog,
> Adder's fork, and blind-worm's sting,

Lizard's leg, and owlet's wing,—
For a charm of powerful trouble,
Like a hell-broth boil and bubble.
Double, double toil and trouble;
Fire burn, and caldron bubble.

So what was this powerful witch's brew made of, a brew which includes tongue of dog? In fact each of the ingredients is a plant and not the part of an animal, least of all a dog. The eye of newt was a common name for mustard seed; the toe of frog was buttercup; the wool of bat was holly leaves; adders fork was the dogtooth violet; blind-worm was slow-worm; and tongue of dog refers to houndstongue, a highly toxic plant which can grow up to four feet tall, has long hairy stalks and has clumps of purplish flowers at the ends of the stems.

I TOO GREW UP WITH A WITCH

I don't know how to make Shakespeare's or any other witch's potion and nor—at least to my best knowledge—have I met a practising witch. But I did know Miss Lindsay.

Miss Lindsay ran the little village shop and post office in a very small village near Oxford. She was already getting old when I was a child of five or so. Or perhaps she just seemed old because her hair was silver and held back with a narrow black velvet ribbon so different from my mother's hair which was brown and permed. But then of course my mother was young and up to date in the 1950's.

We walked along a footpath beside a field and I picked a bunch of wild flowers to present to Miss Lindsay as a thank-you for the toffee or fruit drop which she would give me from one of the large glass jars on the shelf behind the counter. She appreciated flowers and often invited us to have tea in her back garden. The shop being the front room of her house, we just had to go through a door next to the sweet jars and along a dark corridor out into her garden where the abundance of flowers and herbs in multiple colours overflowed from the flowerbeds. I sat on a tiny patch of grass making daisy chains nibbling biscuits from a pretty little plate while she and my mother relaxed in deckchairs chatting and drinking tea.

Miss Lindsay was not married and had no children or family. She lived alone in her village cottage. Around 1970 the rather grand title of postmistress was taken from her by the authorities because she had begun to confuse the money in the post office till with the money in the shop till in order to give her customers the correct change. A new village shop and post office was opened to replace hers. I remember my mother being upset that there was nobody to look after Miss Lindsay. 'But then', said my mother 'Miss Lindsay would never have coped with decimalisation!'

But Miss Lindsay kept going. With no shop to run, she took to walking the countryside in all weathers, a tall thin figure in a long black coat and hat, brandishing a walking stick.

It was not until years later when I stopped to read the names on the modest village war memorial of those killed in the First World War that I realised that there were four Lindsays, her father and three brothers, listed along with most of the men living in the parish at the time. Perhaps, I thought, she was engaged to one of those young men.

Miss Lindsay became increasingly eccentric and I was reminded of her again when I heard that the local children said she was a witch when they saw her tramping in the fields. It made me sad to think she was misunderstood; I preferred to think she was gathering herbs and other wild produce from the hedgerows to spice up the vegetables from her garden. I can easily imagine she would have made a fine brew from unusual ingredients for her supper. But perhaps the children were right, and she really was a charming witch. If so she would surely have been a white witch.

Deborah Kaplinsky, Early Years Teacher (Retired)
London, UK

This Book is NOT

Witchcraft seems to arrive in short bursts every century. We don't know whether these events involved the benign or the malign kind of witches. Lets see what happens in the 2060s. But don't hold your breath. Witches are notoriously unreliable.

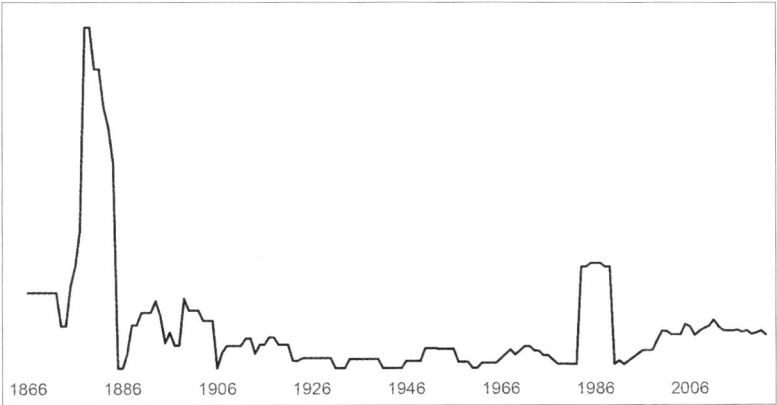

MEAN AS A JUNKYARD DOG

JUNKYARD? Who would want to live in one? A mess, a shambles of discarded and unwanted objects, and generally objects which have no value. And, more often than not, a junkyard can be a dangerous place—rusting metal, potentially hazardous chemicals. Worthless detritus to stumble over, muck to ruin your clothes and chemicals to injure your health.

What sort of dog would bother to defend a junkyard? A vicious dog, with snarling mouth and almost certainly large and fierce, perhaps even restrained by a metal leash. You wouldn't want to meet a junkyard dog in the dark of night, or nor for that matter in light of day. So to refer to someone as being like a junkyard dog is therefore hardly a compliment. They are likely to be combative and aggressive, and dangerously protective of their possessions. Keep out of their way—they are trouble. You might even want to use this phrase to describe the current American president, or perhaps he might be better described as 'meaner than a junkyard dog'…

It is difficult to trace the origins of this idiom. It's a distinctively American phrase—the image is of a scrapyard of old cars, piled high, protected by a vicious Alsation or Rottweiler, redolent of run-down downtown lots in the '50s and '60s. In 1973 Jim Croce wrote the song 'Bad, Bad, Leroy Brown' describing Leroy Brown as 'badder than old King Kong, and meaner than a junk yard dog'. During the '80s and '90s an American wrestler Sylvester Ritter used the moniker *The Junkyard Dog*, wearing a dog collar just in case his educated audience missed the point. Ritter was the first Afro-American with a major presence in this sport, and proved to be a massive draw-card. Part of his storyline was that since he was blinded in a tag-wrestling match by his opponents the Fabulous Freebirds he would only be able to hold his new baby and not see her. One of his fans was about to take revenge and shoot the Fabulous Freebirds from a ringside seat when Ritter was saved from proving a magical recovery from loss of site by the intervening Security. Of course this and similar stories all added to the mystique of *The Junkyard Dog*.

                                            This Book is NOT

JUNKYARD DOG?

I've never actually met a junkyard dog. Many years ago I used to frequent scrapyards when it was still possible to replace damaged metal body panels with less rusty ones from a scrapped car. Instead, it was the scrap metal dealers themselves you had to watch out for. Most of the time, they would routinely try to rip you off by trying to charge you the going rate for a new door or bonnet, purely as a matter of principle. You also had to keep a wary eye out whilst you were struggling to unbolt the part you wanted from your chosen wreck of your particular marque, which was quite often balanced precariously on top of another one of the same make or model. Meanwhile, your friendly local scrap merchant would be busily moving wrecked cars or constituent parts around you or over your head by crane, tractor or forklift. Health and safety? Didn't exist in traditional British scrapyards in the early eighties.

Most scrap dealers were too tight to pay for the minimal upkeep required to keep even the meanest, mangiest mutt alive and snarling. Which is not to say they may not have existed in other scrapyards outside of Sussex—but certainly within the working hours of daylight it wouldn't have made good business sense for them to have their paying customers savaged before they were able to hand over their ready cash. British scrap merchants were truly enlightened and customer-focused capitalist entrepreneurs long before the concept of pre-owned component recycling specialist retailers had been invented—and at least a decade before Del Boy and Rodney had seen the light of televisual day.

But when I cleared my late brother's house thirteen years ago, among his mass of musical memorabilia and numerous stringed instruments was a Jim Croce Greatest Hits songbook, complete with words, lyrics and musical notation for guitar. I don't remember 'Leroy Brown' being one of his compositions but as an accomplished blues guitarist my brother definitely performed it. I have his version on cassette tape here somewhere; this was before home recording to CD was even a thing. He recorded it with his blues-folk group of the time, which was just him and two female singers, whose harmonies were sublime. (Think Agnetha and Frida but without the lurex jumpsuits or quite so many number one hit

There was a time between 1970 and the early 2000s when junkyards flourished. We paid more attention to the environment and reused parts from scrap cars rather than splashing out on new spares and cars. But we then seem to have lost our resolution after 2005. Or perhaps the real reason for these trends is that rottweilers were banned from patrolling junkyards?

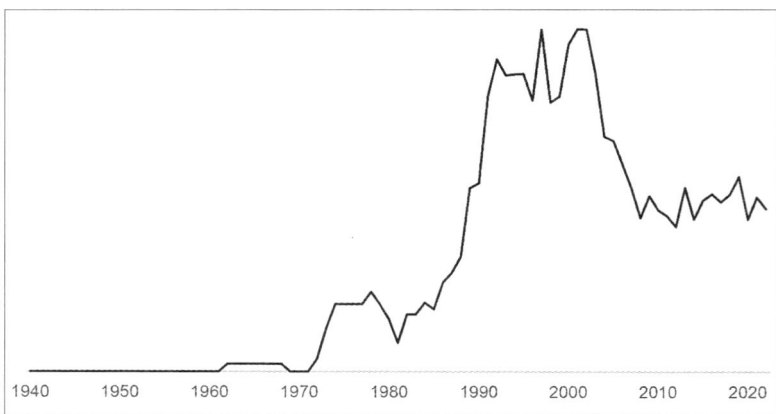

BLACK DOG

DEPRESSION APPARENTLY looks a little different in Europe and North America when compared with India. In the western world, if you have been really low for an extended period, you may feel as if you have been relentlessly tracked by a black dog. (As one mind-focused website, betterhelp.com, explains insightfully, 'Note that 'Black Dog' is a metaphor. If you are seeing a black dog that is not visible to others... reach out to a therapist or psychiatrist for further guidance with managing this symptom'). On the other hand, if you really are being followed by a black dog (your own labrador?) that does not necessarily mean you are depressed.

Famously, Winston Churchill, who was prone to extended periods of melancholy, described these dark passages in his personal life as being visited by his 'black dog'. Luckily his own dog was a brown poodle called Rufus who he took with him on the hazardous trips across the Atlantic to meet the American president. But perhaps Churchill was less admiring of President Roosevelt than it seemed, since Rufus was not allowed to enter the Cabinet Room in London. Rufus was run over by a car in 1947 and his successor, Rufus II, was buried with Churchill.

The association between black dogs and depression is widespread in western culture. In 65 BC Horace wrote of 'black dog depression'. In English folklore the black dog was associated with the devil. It was seen as an omen of death and dark forces. For example, a notorious nobleman in Dartmoor, Richard Cabell was said to have sold his soul to the devil and at his death in 1677, black dogs appeared at his burial chamber. This fable inspired Conan Doyle's *The Hound of the Baskervilles*. In Belgium, the Beast of Flanders was a large black dog with fierce red eyes; in Germany and Czech territory the devil appeared as a black dog and in Italy a large black dog tried to steal the mystic Benedetta Carlini when she was a child. Influenced by the culture of Spanish and Italian invaders, it was widely believed in Mexico, Argentina and Paraguay that the devil was a shape-changing sorcerer who appeared sometimes as a black dog.

Not surprisingly the metaphorical link between black dogs and dark forces surfaces in English literature. Perhaps Conan Doyle's *The Hound of the Baskervilles* (1902) was influenced by a short story by WHC Pynchon (grandfather of the well-known novelist Thomas Pynchon) written in 1898 which contained the admonition 'And if a man shall meet the Black Dog once it shall be for joy; and if twice, it shall be for sorrow; and the third time he shall die'. More recently, Ian McEwan's controversial 1992 novel *Black Dogs* is centred around the fall of the Berlin Wall in 1989 and the underbelly of Nazism which continues to exist in rural France. And turning to high culture, a black dog haunts churchyards and is an omen of death in a number of Harry Potter novels.

It must surely be due to living in different hemispheres, but unlike western culture where the black dog is frequently seen as a dark force and a symbol of depression, in Hindu culture the black dog is a positive force. If you confront problems due to the bad positioning of Shina in the astrological world, keeping a black dog at home will provide protection and relief since both Saturn and Ketu are affected by black-coloured dogs. But make sure you keep your dog in the north, north-east or north-western position. And if a black dog follows you on your way home, good luck to you.

BLACK DOGS? NOT MY PROBLEM

I have never thought of my depression as a black dog or a dog of any colour—or any animal other than a viciously human one. Hell, as we know, is other people. Dogs are a remedy, a relief, an escape—but only if you actually like dogs, I suppose. I'd never considered Churchill to be a dog person in the first place and I hold it against him to have perpetuated and popularised this image of a dog as worrying tormentor. Subconsciously, I think I'd always thought of him as more of a cat person anyway, which would surely have been a good thing for a wartime prime minister pitted against such a warmongering, teetotal vegetarian psychopath as Madolf Hoodlum. Hitler remained besotted with his Alsatian, Blondie, right until

This Book is NOT

their end in the Berlin bunker. If anyone was to have given a dog a bad name, it should rightly have been Hitler and not Churchill, and anyway, Hitler's Alsatian was brown.

Maybe if I'd ever been bitten by a dog or even seriously frightened by one I might feel differently about it? Heaven knows I've given enough dogs enough opportunities to bite me over the years but none have ever found it necessary to do so. Perhaps being taught from a young age to have respect for them and treat them with kindness in the first place has made that difference.

Depression is not something you can easily describe, give a name, a form or a substance to. It might help some people to imagine it in the shape of a creature to be confronted and defeated. But it is a shape-shifter; whether as a phantom or a nameless terror you may think you've seen it off—but the smallest setback can bring it charging back at you from any and every direction, sometimes in a series of small crises in close succession, sometimes overwhelmingly and all at once like a crushing avalanche.

Just trying to describe it—to a blissful non-sufferer—by putting it down in words is like nailing fog to the wall; even as I type this it is looking over my shoulder, breathing down my neck, whispering 'Remember me?' And it's most definitely not a dog; a dog would be sitting at my feet, looking adoringly up at me and thumping its tail on the floor, reminding me that it's time for a walk—and how about looking in at the pub where the lovely bar staff give away dog treats?

So as a long-term depressive, currently off medication and feeling better for it, having gone cold turkey several years ago whilst helping my sister-in-law to move house the week before Christmas—if anything was going to cause a serious relapse it would have been that kind of stressful experience. Fortunately, she had two lovely dogs, a loony collie and a mischievous terrier—thank you, Jess and Mollie.

So I'm sorry, Winnie, you were wrong—though I'm not going to suggest that Adolf was right—not even regarding his choice of pets.

Clive Hobden, Sussex Police Force
Lewes, UK

Poor old Conan Doyle. Far from *The Hound of the Baskervilles* leading to an increase in references to 'black dogs', the opposite seems to have occurred. By contrast, good on you Ian McEwan. And acknowledgement also to Winston Churchill whose black dog experiences seem to have been contagious.

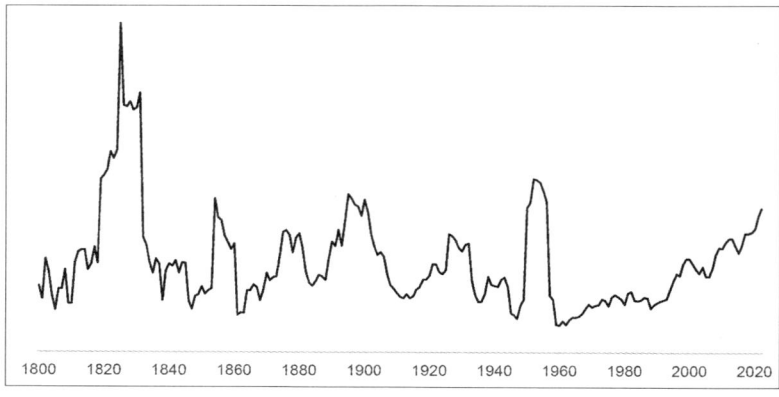

This Book is NOT

HOT DOG

MOST METAPHORS have a single meaning. Some well-endowed metaphors may have two, or even three different meanings. But spare a thought for hot dog. Greens' Dictionary of Slang provides seventeen alternatives, including nouns, verbs, adjectives and exclamations. So as James Lamour helpfully points out, the string 'Hot dog! A hot-dog hot dog, a hot-dog hot dog and that other hot-dog hot dogger hot-dogged those hot dogs from that hot doggery, but during a hot dog, one slipped on that dog's hot dog'. This translates as 'Whoa! A flamboyant gay dude, a good, successful gambler and that other greedy show-off grabbed those frankfurters from that sausage cart, but during a chase, one slipped on that pup's poo. What an idiot'.

Sausages are as old as humankind's transition to settled agriculture in the 9th century BC. The meat of slaughtered animals needed to be preserved. Encasing it in the intestines of slaughtered animals turned out to be an effective means of storage. But of course, not all sausages are identical. In the late seventeenth century, a butcher in Coburg Germany called Johan Georghehner 'invented' a sausage which he said looked like a dachshund dog. Excited by his culinary 'delicacy', he took this to Frankfurt, where it proved to be a hit and rapidly spread throughout Europe. Then in the late 19th century, German migrants brought the frankfurter to the US. And the rest is, as they say, history.

Sausage, originally spelt *sawsyge* entered the English language in the mid-15th century. It originated from old north French *saussiche* which in turn was drawn from the Latin *salsica*.

The National Hot Dog and Sausage Council of America estimated that in 2022 Americans purchased nine billion hot dogs from grocery stores and consumed a further 11 billion hot dogs in eateries, baseball parks and other social events. Wouldn't Johan Georghehner be proud! The hot dog is quintessentially an American 'delicacy' (although this might be stretching the word delicacy to its limits), but the global spread of the American Dream pushes the annual global consumption of frankfurters to extraordinary numbers. Not so many frankfurters as grains of sand on the seashore, but ubiquitous, nevertheless.

The annual 4th July Hot Dog Eating Contest in New York 2022 saw Joey Chestnut winning for the sixteenth time. He managed to consume 62 of the delicacies in ten minutes. But it seems that poor Joey may have been put off by a lightning strike which hospitalised two passing pedestrians, since this winning margin was some distance from his world record of 76 hot dogs in ten minutes. The multiple female prize winner Miki Sudo won her ninth title, guzzling 39 and a half hot dogs in the allotted ten minutes. Surely Johan Georghehner was dancing in his grave with pride.

HOT DOG LUNCH

'Hot dog!', the boy yelled, excitedly pulling on his mother's arm and pointing at the long, burnished-red sausage dog trotting alongside me. 'Pleeeaaaase, can we get one?', the boy intones, alternating longing looks at the dog and pleading eyes on his mother. With a long-suffering look, the mother responds, 'No Jake, we are not getting a sausage dog'.

It is with a mix of amusement and indignation that this scene plays out, as we walk our miniature dachshund along the waterfront. Amusement comes from the delight people get from seeing our misshapen dog—long body, short legs—trotting along, 16 steps for every one of ours. She is literally a smile machine, as person after person breaks out in a broad grin as they spot her. The indignation comes from the words that then come out of their mouth, 'Aww, a sausage!'

My gorgeous hot dog is not your lunch.

...

'Hot dog!', the boy yelled, excitedly pulling on his mother's arm and pointing at the long, burnished-red sausage on the sign at the hot dog stand. 'Pleeeaaaase, can we get one?, the boy intones, alternating longing looks at the hot dog and pleading eyes on his mother.

My son is three-years old. We are on holiday in Australia—perhaps not the original home of the hot dog, but a close relation. There is a hot dog stand. Steaming, long sausages cooking on a grill. Soft buns, just the right length, and slit down the middle. Squeezy bottles of tomato sauce and mustard. There is something tantalizing about the first bite of a hot dog. Whether it is the slight resistance as your teeth cut through the collagen coating (the days of intestine stockings now gone), or the salty-smoky taste of the sausage itself. Yes, my son could try his first hot dog.

We place our order—tomato sauce, but no mustard, he decides. 'Here you go, young man!', says the vendor, grinning as he hands my son his prize. My son carries it reverently to a nearby picnic table, passing it to me for safe keeping as he clambers onto the bench seat. He turns to retrieve the hot dog from me, as I slide onto the seat opposite him. His grin is only just visible over the top of the picnic table, but his eyes are sparkling in anticipation. His little arms reach up, grasping the hot dog in both hands, and bringing it into position just below his chin. So careful not to drop it. A last beam as he readies himself to bite… at which moment, the sausage vanishes. An ibis bird, with its long, curved beak had reached up under the table, and plucked the sausage from its bun. One swift manoeuvre and the hot dog was gone…

Turns out that gorgeous hot-dog wasn't my son's lunch either.

…

'Hot dog!', thought the long, burnished-red sausage dog, staring at the BBQ, the grill sizzling gently in the afternoon sun. 'Oh, how I want one', she thought, as she contemplated the length of her diminutive legs and the towering height of the BBQ. She alternated longing looks between the sizzling sausage, and the young boy standing next to the BBQ.

Needs must, thought the dog, and turned her pleading eyes on the boy. 'Oh look, mum, she wants a cuddle', the boy said, gathering the dog tenderly into his arms and standing up, proffering the dog like a prize. The wily sausage let the 'oohs' and 'aahs' play out for a moment, biding her time. Then she struck—neck extended, teeth engaged, tongue like a lasso, and plucked the hot dog from the grill.

Polly Schaverian, Clinical Psychologist
Wellington, New Zealand.

Poor Johan Georghehner. He may have invented the frankfurter in the late 1600s, but it was only in the 20th century that references to hot dog surfaced in publications. This fame reached its peak in the early 2000s, and was followed by a sharp decline. Have culinary tastes really improved, or are hot dogs so numerous that we no longer bother to mention their presence? Like the air and sand, they just ARE.

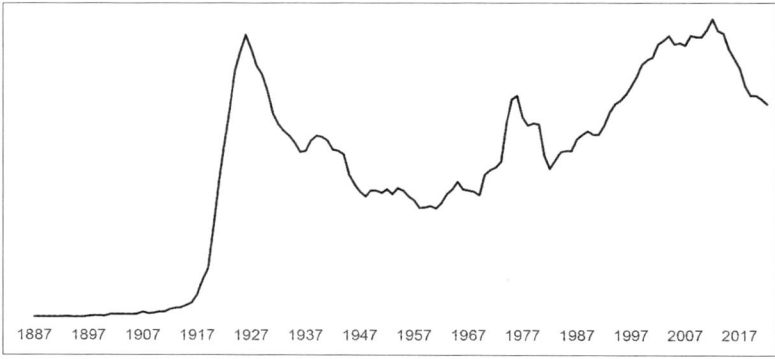

This Book is NOT

A DOG IS MAN'S BEST FRIEND

MOST IDIOMS are metaphors or similes. Both paint a picture by comparing unlike things. A metaphor requires more work of the listener, providing an indirect comparison between two apparently different things. By contrast the simile does the hard work for you, telling you directly that one thing is 'like' another.

But sometimes an aphorism does not ask you to compare like with unlike, it just tells you what things are. And this is the case for the aphorism that a dog is man's best friend. Because in fact a dog IS man's best friend.

Two thousand years ago in Ancient Greece, Homer knew this. He tells the story of King Odysseus' return from the Trojan War to Ithaca. The only 'person' to recognise him is his beloved dog, Argos.

As they [Eumaeus and Ulysses] were thus talking, a dog that had been lying asleep raised his head and pricked up his ears. This was Argos, whom Ulysses had bred before setting out for Troy… In the old days he used to be taken out by the young men when they went hunting wild goats, or deer, or hares, but now that his master was gone he was lying neglected on the heaps of mule and cow dung that lay in front of the stable doors till the men should come and draw it away to manure the great close; and he was full of fleas. As soon as he saw Ulysses standing there, he dropped his ears and wagged his tail, but he could not get close up to his master. When Ulysses saw the dog on the other side of the yard, dashed a tear from his eyes without Eumaeus seeing it, and said:

'Eumaeus, what a noble hound that is over yonder on the manure heap: his build is splendid; is he as fine a fellow as he looks, or is he only one of those dogs that come begging about a table, and are kept merely for show?'

'This hound', answered Eumaeus, 'belonged to him who has died in a far country. If he were what he was when Ulysses left for Troy, he would soon show you what he could do. There was not a wild beast in the forest that could get away from him when he was once on its tracks. But now he has fallen on evil times, for his master is dead and gone, and the women take no care of him.'

1,500 years later in the mid-18th century, the king of Prussia, Frederick II, famously referred to one of his Italian greyhounds as his best friend and this if often taken to be the origin of this phrase.

As dogs transitioned from their roles as hunters, trackers, watchers, protectors and guards, so they increasingly morphed into the firmest of friends. The American poet, Ogden Nash knew this, and in 1941 wrote a poem entitled 'An Introduction to Dogs':

The dog is man's best friend.
He has a tail on one end.
Up in front, he has teeth.
And four legs underneath.

Dogs like to bark.
They like it best after dark.
They not only frighten prowlers away
But also hold the sandman at bay.

A dog that is indoors
To be let out implores.
You let him out and what then?
He wants back in again.

Dogs display reluctance and wrath
If you try to give them a bath.
They bury bones in hideaways
And half the time they trot sideways.

Dogs in the country have fun.
They run and run and run.
But in the city this species
Is dragged around on leashes.

Dogs are upright as a steeple
And much more loyal than people.
Well people may be reprehensibler
But that's probably because they are sensibler.

And if you don't believe Ogden Nash, then perhaps you might be persuaded by a famous court case in America in 1869. The owner of a black and tan coonhound named 'Old Drum' sued a neighbour for shooting his dog and the case was eventually heard by the US Supreme Court. The long testimony by George Graham Vest, the prosecuting lawyer has become famous and is known as 'Eulogy to a Dog':

Gentlemen of the jury, the best friend a man has in this world may turn against him and become his enemy. His son or daughter whom he has reared with loving care may prove ungrateful. Those who are nearest and dearest to us—those whom we trust with our happiness and good name—may become traitors in their faith. The money that a man has he may lose. It flies away from him, perhaps when he needs it most. A man's reputation may be sacrificed in a moment of ill-considered action. The people who are prone to fall on their knees to do us honour when success is with us may be the first to throw the stone of malice when failure settles its cloud upon our heads. The one absolute, unselfish friend that man can have in this selfish world—the one that never proves ungrateful or treacherous—is his dog.

Gentlemen of the jury, a man's dog stands by him in prosperity and poverty, in health and sickness. He will sleep on the cold ground, where the wintry winds blow, and the snow drives fiercely, if only he can be near his master's side. He will kiss the hand that has no food to offer; he will lick the wounds and sores that come in encounter with the roughness of the world. He guards the sleep of his pauper master as if he were a prince. When all other friends desert, he remains. When riches take wings and reputation falls to pieces, he is as constant in his love as the sun in its journey through the heavens.

If fortune drives the master forth an outcast in the world, friendless and homeless, the faithful dog asks no higher privilege than that of accompanying him to guard against danger, to fight against his enemies. And when the last scene of all comes, and death takes the master in its embrace, and his body is laid away in the cold ground, no matter if all other friends pursue their way, there by his graveside will the noble dog be found, his head between his paws, his eyes sad but open in alert watchfulness, faithful and true even to death.'

There is a bronze statue to Old Drum outside the courtroom where Vest presented the case for prosecution.

FINNEY AND HACHIKO CARRY THE FLAG

And if you still don't believe the absolute truth that a dog is indeed man's best friend, then consider the case of Rich Moore, aged 71 and his Jack Russell terrier, Finney. Finney was adopted as the runt of a litter in 2020. Moore set off with his two-year old companion to climb Blackhead Peak (12,500 foot high) in Colorado on the 19th August 2023. He never returned He evidently fell and died of hypothermia during the cold mountain nights. Helicopters and 176 volunteers combed the mountain for 16 days in the largest search-and-rescue operation mounted in the area. But they found no trace of his body. Ten weeks later, on the 30th October, a hunter found Finney guarding his owner's dead body. He weighed less than six pounds, half of his original body weight. Jack Russell are fiercesome and brave and Finney had managed to keep roaming mountain lions, coyotes and bears away from the body for all that time. He seemed to have survived by eating small rodents and moths and insects (this is what he has been ferreting for since his return home). He now also wakes up for biscuits four or five times a night, no doubt after nightmares. So, no question—Finney was demonstrably Rich Moore's best friend.

Finney's recent fame pales into insignificance when compared to a 41kg Japanese Akita dog called Hachiko. He was born in November 1923 and was adopted by a Japanese professor in 1924. With amazing regularity and time-keeping Hachiko would make his way to the railway station to meet his returning master every evening. But his owner died suddenly of a cerebral hemorrhage during a lecture, and the eighteen month old Hiraki was heartbroken. He continued to remain his master's best friend and every evening for the next nine years, nine months and fifteen days, Hiraki visited the train station at the same time to 'greet' his master, nourished by food and treats brought to him by admiring citizens.

Hachiko became a national symbol of loyalty. When he died at the age of 11, he was buried next to his owner. A number of monuments have been constructed in his honour and every year there is a remembrance ceremony at an exit to the Shibuya railway station which is named after Hachiko. In 1994 engineers managed to revive a record of Hachiko's bark from a broken 78 RPM vinyl record, which was broadcast to millions of radio listeners. In 2009 a tear-jerking version of Hachiko's story was transfigured into an American setting in a movie called Hachi: A Dogs Tail. See it and weep.

Raphie Kaplinsky
Development Economist (Retired)

The power of Hollywood can be seen in the spike in references to a dog is a man's best friend after the film *Hachi: A Dogs Tail* was released in 2009. But as for the spike during the 1970s... only man's best friend might know the answer to that question.

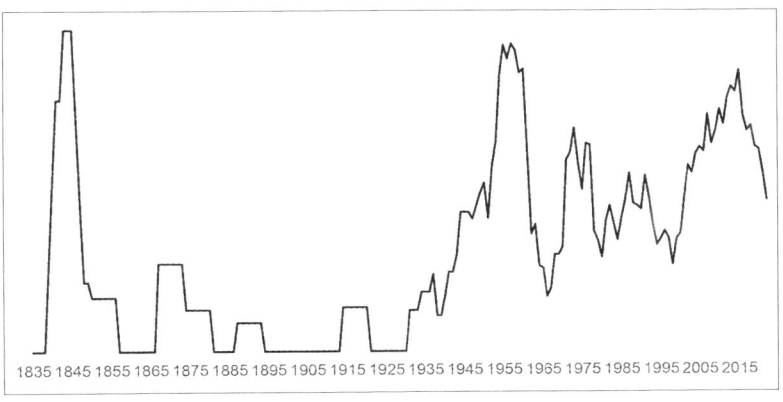